CLASS OF "55"

Bruce Nieban
10-1-05

Splinters

Splinters

*The Story of
a Lumber Company,
a Loving Family,
a Living Church,
a Loyal Community*

By Bernie Niehaus

*Chairman of the Board
The Niehaus Companies
Vincennes, Indiana*

Printed by Abbey Press,
St. Meinrad, IN, USA

Cover and book design by Scott Wannemuehler, GrafixStudio, Inc.

Acknowledgements

The author wishes to acknowledge the able editing assistance of Linus Mundy, publisher of Abbey Press, for his help. Linus serves on the Board of Overseers with me and has been a great Saint Meinrad friend for many years. He has written many *CareNotes* and several books including *PrayerWalking— A Simple Path to Body-and-Soul Fitness*.

Thanks also to Scott Wannemuehler, of GrafixStudio, Inc. for his energy and talent in designing this book and cover. His graphic expertise makes the pictures and text come to life.

Finally, thanks to Sherry Cummins, Advertising/Marketing Manager of Niehaus Companies, Inc., for her diligence and devotion to this book. This book would not have been possible without her persistence and many hours of help.

About the Author

Bernard G. Niehaus is CEO of Niehaus Companies, located in Vincennes, Indiana. Bernie grew up in the lumber business and joined the family business full-time after completing his education in 1959.

Bernie is an alumnus of Saint Meinrad having spent three of his high school years there. He received an Associate Degree at Vincennes University, and a BS Degree in Lumber Merchandising, from Michigan State University. After completing college, he took the helm of the family business and started making changes, and the business began to grow. By 2003, the company had grown to include three businesses at six locations: Niehaus Home Center, Wholesale Building Materials in Vincennes, St. Louis, Nashville, Tennessee, and the Big Buck Building Centers in Robinson, Illinois and Terre Haute, Indiana. The company includes a Therma-Tru door manufacturing plant and a counter top manufacturing plant. Niehaus Companies also includes an importing division, Karran USA, which distributes solid surface sinks and whirlpools. The company also has an engineered lumber design and sales center.

Bernie has been very active in his community and has been generous with his time and resources by heading up fund raising organizations to help schools, churches, charity groups, and several community betterment groups. He served on the Board of Trustees at Vincennes University for 23 years and 4 years as Chairman of the Board. He was instrumental in implementing new construction projects and programs at the University. He has served as President, Regional Director, and the Executive Committee of the Indiana Lumberman's Building Supply Association. He has served as Director of the American National Bank and AMBANC Corporation, as a Director and on the Board of First Federal Savings and Loan. He served as Secretary of the New Vincennes Area Industrial Development Committee and Vice-President of the Christian Education Foundation. He is past Chairman of the Board of Overseers at St. Meinrad's School of Theology and past Chairman of the Board of the Catholic Foundation for the Diocese of Evansville.

He and his wife, Patty, are the parents of five children—two daughters and three sons. The three sons now hold positions in the company. Butch is now President, David, Vice-President of Sales, and Eric is Vice-President of Operations.

Bernie and Patty are the proud grandparents of 19 grandchildren.

Dedication

This book is dedicated to my family—because my family is the reason for this book.

I want them to know about the generations before them and the love we all share.

My wife—Patty O'Neill Niehaus
My Mother—Naomi Niehaus
My children, their spouses and their children—
    Anne Niehaus Pratt & Robert Pratt
        Brennan, Julia, Alec and Kevin
    Butch Niehaus & Tina
        Mallory, Nicholas, Megan and Molly
    Catherine Niehaus Lawless & Steve Lawless
        Jensen, Johnny and Mickey
    David Niehaus & Maggie
        Emily, Ben, Katie and Abby
    Eric Niehaus & Teresa
        Bailey, Jackson, Natalie and Charlie
My sister, her husband & their children—
    Sondra Niehaus Glennon & Tim Glennon
    Michael Glennon
    Danny Glennon & Margarette
        Mary Elizabeth and Joey

Contents

Foreword

There's hardly anybody at Saint Meinrad Archabbey and Seminary who doesn't know Bernie Niehaus. There are a number of us who know him from the days when he was here as a student. There are many who know him because he's here frequently visiting and serves on the Board of Overseers and other committees.

Bernie came here as a young man thinking God wanted him to be a priest. He discovered that God did not want him to be a priest. But Saint Meinrad education gave him something and this has dramatically influenced his life. Saint Meinrad gave him a way of viewing the world, a way of offering himself fully to the call that God had in mind for him: the call to be husband, father, businessman, and authentic Christian in the workaday world.

Bernie knows that he got a lot at Saint Meinrad, and he is one who is extremely appreciative. And so, hearing that he is doing this book, I'm thrilled to be able to commend him as one who brings to the business world a sense of true Christian stewardship. Every page of this history of his lumber company has exuding from it an ethic which is example to business employers and employees alike. We salute Bernie as he recalls the history of this lumber company, and we're glad that in some way there's a bit of influence in how he deals with his employees and customers that has come his way from farther south in Indiana.

Congratulations, Bernie. We're proud of you as an alumnus and we salute you and your accomplishments.

Rt. Rev. Lambert Reilly, OSB
Archabbot

Chapter 1
The Beginning

"...he began to sell roofing, cement and other building materials—thus, the beginning of Niehaus Home Center."

The Early Years

From *Niehaus News*, February, 2001

The Niehaus family has been involved in the lumber and building materials business for almost 100 years now. In *Green's History of Vincennes and Knox County* it states that Benjamin Niehaus in 1906 was Secretary-Treasurer of Vincennes Sash and Door Company. He was also described in Green's History as the head of an interesting and intelligent family. The Sash and Door Company was located on Lyndale Avenue, where an apartment house now stands.

Father Niehaus, my father's brother, told about working in the plant during the summer of his seminary days in the 1920's. He recalled delivering window sashes and doors with a horse-drawn wagon. He also spoke about how the plant machinery was run on steam and the belts from the main power wheel ran all over the plant.

Somewhere in the 1920's, Grandpa Niehaus (Benjamin) bought a sawmill in Tennessee. He would send loads of rough lumber back to this area. Father Niehaus also tells the story about how he and his brother, Alfred, got malaria while working in Tennessee and had to be sent home.

In 1933 Benjamin Niehaus and Francis Niehaus opened Niehaus Planing Mill at our present location on Main Street. Clayton Miller, one of their first employees, stated that his workbench was in the front window facing Main Street, directly across from the Ohenemus Saloon. On his work bench, Clayton talks of building kitchen cabinets, window units, and door frames.

Benjamin Niehaus was an inventive sort and very skilled with mill machinery. He made a lot of items for the farmers like binder rollers for wheat farmers, hot bed sash and wood crates for the melon farmers. Francis, my father, worked in the office and began to sell roofing, cement, and other building materials—thus, the beginning of Niehaus Home Center.

The grandchildren, great grandchildren, and now great-great grandchildren of Benjamin Niehaus, hope to live in Knox County much in the same way his life was described in Green's History (1911) "in the enjoyment of all that make life most desirable."

Benjamin Niehaus, co-founder of Niehaus Lumber Company, Grandfather of Bernie Niehaus.

Clayton Miller—First employee hired at Niehaus Lumber Company in 1933.

Francis Niehaus, co-founder of Niehaus Lumber Company, holding his son, Bernie. Circa 1938.

"I will always be grateful to my mother who held on to our family business during those critical years."

The Critical Years

From *Niehaus News*, March, 2001

In last month's Splinters, I talked about the early years of our Niehaus family business from 1906 – 1933. I label the years 1933 – 1959, the "critical years." In 1933, right in the middle of the Depression, my father and grandfather opened up Niehaus Planing Mill at 11th and Main Streets, where our new Home Center is today. My grandfather told the story about sprinkling sawdust and shavings around on the floor to make it look like they were busy.

After surviving the depression years, World War II in the early 1940's made it very hard to get lumber. My grandpa would go on mill trips to buy the lumber for us. I went on several of these trips with him. This was my first introduction to the lumber business.

They needed this lumber for our mill shop where they made kitchen cabinets, door frames and windows—all beginning with rough cut lumber. Francis would order truck loads of roofing, cement and building materials for resale. This became the most successful part of the business, as the need for custom mill work began to fade away.

In November of 1944, at the age of 36, my father died of tuberculosis. His untimely death left a void in the retail lumber business. To fill the void, Naomi Niehaus, the young widow and mother of two small children, came to work in the office to carry on Francis' position. I was just seven and my sister Sondra was six years of age. My mother had a difficult task ahead. Being a woman in the lumber business was a very rare circumstance in those days. With a firm purpose and unfaltering determination, the business grew.

In 1959, I graduated from Michigan State University with a Bachelor of Science Degree in Lumber Merchandising. After graduation I joined the family lumber business. I will always be grateful to my mother who held on to our family business during those critical years.

Mrs. Naomi Niehaus and her children, Sondra and Bernie, at the graveside of their father.

Bernie and his sister Sonie, with their grandfather, Ben Niehaus, one year after their father's death—1945.

One of the first payroll books showing the weekly salaries of employees in 1937.

"...our first millwork and cabinet plant on Lyndale Avenue."

The Niehaus Family—100 Years in Cabinets

From *Niehaus News*, February, 2002

Over 100 years ago somewhere in the late 1890's, my grandfather, Benjamin Niehaus and August Schultheis, left Haubstadt, Indiana and came to Vincennes to start a furniture, cabinet, and millwork company. The Nash & May Manufacturing Co. was located on Lyndale Avenue.

My grandfather and two of his sons, Francis (my father) and Alfred (who later started Niehaus Electric) were very skilled cabinet makers. They all three worked in the mill of the Knox County Lumber Company in the late 1920's. In 1933 they started Niehaus Lumber Co., whose primary business was planing rough lumber for the farmers, millwork and cabinets.

In the late forties, when I was in grad school, I would help off-bear the big planer, which created huge mounds of sawdust and wood shavings. I also remember six to eight carpenters working at their benches with a set of kitchen cabinets in the making. Each man would pick out the material from the large rough lumber stack. He would then take it to the joiner to straighten the edges before ripping it on the table saw. All the joints on the cabinets were mortise and tenon. Several people have told me that they still have the cabinets we made for them in the 30's and 40's.

In 1959 after graduating from Michigan State, I came back to the family business. At that time, I saw that stock cabinets were starting to come on. We started handling Scheirch cabinets made in Louisville. In 1959 we opened our first kitchen department for Niehaus Lumber and Eldon Campbell was the first manager. By 1962, we started to buy from a small cabinet company in Jasper, Indiana called United Cabinet. After a few years they became Aristokraft and now are a part of MasterBrand, one of the largest kitchen cabinet manufacturers in the country.

Our relationship with Aristokraft has been a very special and rewarding one. We now distribute their cabinets in five states including St. Louis and Nashville. We are their third largest distributor in the country.

As the feature story of this newsletter indicates, we have just opened up a "state of the art" kitchen and bath design showroom at our Niehaus Home Center. We have come a long way since the first cabinet company in 1904 and first showroom in 1959.

David and Butch Niehaus and Brian Childs (Manager of WBM, St. Louis) observe the festivities at the WBM - Aristokraft 40th Anniversary celebration.

Aristokraft

Bernie Niehaus was presented a plaque by Rich Forbes, President of Master Brands Cabinets, honoring the 40th Anniversary of Niehaus being a distributor of Aristokraft Cabinetry.

The above newspaper ad dated July 4, 1904, was given to Bernie Niehaus by Jane Niehaus. Printing at the top of the ad shows that Bernie's grandfather, Benjamin Niehaus, is the president of the Nash & May Manufacturing Company. The company manufactured a variety of products including cabinetry.

"...smell the resin in the pine boards and think of the days in the old mill and piles of sawdust and shavings"

Sawdust in My Blood

From *Niehaus News*, November, 1999

As far back as I can remember, the smell of sawdust, shavings and freshly planed lumber made my "juices flow," as they say today.

In 1933 my father and grandfather opened Niehaus Planing Mill—what is known today as Niehaus Home Center, which just celebrated its 66th year. In the late 40's when I was in grade school, one of my jobs was to be off-bearer of our huge 24 inch planer. Farmers would bring in their rough sawn lumber—mainly oak or poplar—and we would plane it. At the end of the day the shaving piles were over my head.

We would also go to the sawmills and buy lumber. I remember one trip to Tennessee to buy oak and another trip to Paoli, Indiana, to buy poplar.

After the war, it was easier to get fir and pine from the West Coast. The lumber would come in boxcars loaded to the top. I would climb in the top of the car and push out the boards one at a time. Many times it would take us three or four days to unload a car.

My love for wood took me to Michigan State University's School of Forest Products. While there, I learned Lumber Grading and Preservation. Wood Technology and Dendrology were my favorite courses where we learned to identify the different wood species and trees.

After graduating from Michigan State, I came back to manage our family lumber business. Many other products besides lumber have been added in the last 40 years, but my favorite job is to talk and buy lumber. Over the years, I have made many friends in the lumber industry. One of them, Larry Carter, from Indianapolis, retired last year, but when we get together we still talk about lumber mills and the good old days.

Even today, I can walk down the aisle in our new Home Center and smell the resin in the pine boards and think of the days in the old mill and the piles of sawdust and shavings.

Ken Doades, Assistant Manager at Niehaus Home Center, stocks the pine boards in one of several aisles of lumber.

Bernie Niehaus on his first lumber buying trip to Tennessee with his father and grandfather. Circa 1943.

"The forklift changed the way we did business."

The Watermelon and the Pickle

From *Niehaus News*, August – September, 2002

Back in 1955 when I was a senior in high school, I persuaded my mother to buy a forklift truck. I had been reading in the trade magazines that the mechanical handling of building materials was the future. Up until 1955 we hand-unloaded everything: boxcars of lumber, drywall, and roofing—it was very labor intensive. There were five lumber yards in Vincennes in 1955 and we were one of the smallest. The forklift changed the way we did business. We could now unload cars and trucks in full units instead of pieces. Many of our contractor customers would order in full units. This immediately made us the envy of the other yards in Vincennes and the surrounding area.

This past week Vincennes held its annual Watermelon Festival and this brought back many memories, especially of our first forklift. In the 1950's Vincennes proclaimed itself to be the "Watermelon Capitol of the World," and George Gardner went on national TV to show his skill at spitting watermelon seeds.

In 1956 Vincennes held a Watermelon Festival Parade, so I decided to show off our new forklift in the parade. It was a new, bright yellow Hyster and I was very proud of it.

We needed something for the forklift to do, so we decided it should hold a giant watermelon. A platform was made, and on it we sculptured a watermelon out of chicken wire and plaster of Paris, almost eight feet tall.

I was going to V.U. at the time and had met my wife to be, Patty, and her sister, Betty. They decided to ride on the platform with the beautiful watermelon in the parade.

I was the driver of the forklift, of course, and boy was I proud. As we came down Main Street, we could hear people yell, "Look at the big pickle." Alas, our watermelon looked more like a pickle.

Niehaus Companies Inc., now has 16 forklifts in operation in three of its locations. Shown are six being used at WBM in Vincennes. The drivers are: George Unsworth, Craig Sims, Tim Tamsey, Kyle Blubaum and Mike Montgomery. Absent from the photo is Dennis Bilskie.

Bernie Niehaus with a forklift similar to the one used in the Watermelon Parade in 1955. However, this photo was taken in 1979.

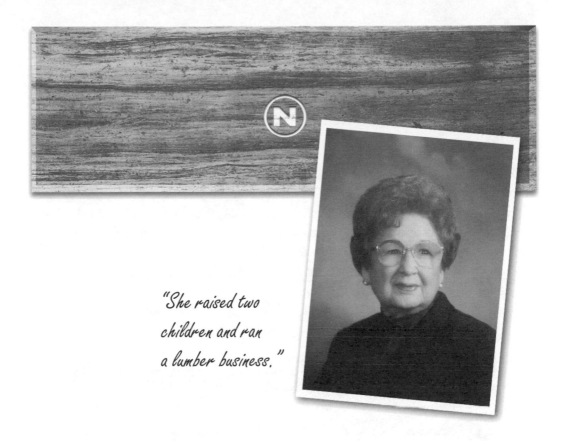

"She raised two children and ran a lumber business."

A Great Lady

From *Niehaus News*, November, 2002

She was an astute businesswoman and a real taskmaster, but for those who know her, she has a soft heart and is generous to a fault. This great lady is my mother. She was widowed at the age of 36. She raised two children and ran a lumber business which was very foreign to women in those days.

I remember that cold, dreary day in November 1944 when Hillcrest Hospital called and said my father had passed away from tuberculosis. My mother had not learned to drive yet, so we called the neighbor next door to take her to the hospital. After my father's death, she was determined to make the business go. She took driving lessons and went to Vincennes Business College for bookkeeping and general business courses.

My sister Sonie and I also had to help during those years. Sonie would help around the house with cooking, cleaning, and laundry. I started my career in the lumber business sweeping sawdust and unloading boxcars of lumber by hand. My mother was very strict and ruled the house with an iron hand or—in actual terms—a plywood paddle she had cut out in our mill.

Sonie and I both feared that paddle for many years.

From 1944 to 1959, she hired several managers to help her with managing the lumber company. One or two of these managers gave her some real problems and I remember well one night her crying—trying to find a new manager.

She is a very soft-hearted person and was even more so with women who had also been widowed. Over the years she hired several of these ladies who were widowed to come work at the lumber company.

I can remember back in 1959 when I got out of college, and she asked me to be president of the lumber company because she thought it was a man's job. I had many ambitious plans to expand our business and she would almost always say yes—because she was my mother, and a Great Lady.

Mrs. Naomi Niehaus at her desk in the early 60's.

Mrs. Naomi Niehaus, mother of Bernie and Sondra Niehaus and President of Niehaus Lumber Company from 1944 to 1959.

"It seems as if history was repeating itself—I was fishing with Ben again—my grandson."

Fishing with Ben

From *Niehaus News*, March, 2003

Seventy years ago my Grandpa Ben and my father Francis started Niehaus Planing Mill. Ben Niehaus was an inventive sort and very skilled with mill machinery. He loved working with the area's farmers. Ben would be down at the mill at 5:30 in the morning turning binder rollers for the wheat farmers and hot bed sashes for the melon farmers, in addition to planing their rough lumber.

As I stated, he was very inventive and sometimes this got him into big trouble. In the 1940's plastic wood for filling holes in wood was just being marketed. Clayton Miller, his long-time mill assistant, told the story about him trying to fix his false teeth with plastic wood. Well, as Clayton explained it, it was quite a mess getting the teeth and the plastic wood out of his mouth.

I remember working in the old mill shop during my grade school and high school years. Ben was a genius with the mill machinery. We had a five-head moulding machine with hundreds of knives on the wall. He would spend half a day setting up this moulding machine with certain knives on the five heads. I always enjoyed watching him run the wide crown mouldings.

In 1944, after my father died, Grandpa became a real part of our family and was a real father figure to me. He lived next to the corner house at 10th and Vigo Streets. So he was a block from the lumber company and two blocks from our house at 10th and Broadway. My mother would invite him to eat Sunday dinner at our house. In the late 1940's, after school one day at the lumber company, Grandpa leaned over and whispered in my ear, "One day you will head up this company."

Grandpa loved to fish, and on many occasions I would go with him. He had one favorite fishing hole—Rusch's Pond—out by St. Thomas. It was owned by Louie and Betty Rusch. He would always call Betty before he went fishing. This last fall it seems as if history was repeating itself down at Kentucky Lake. I was fishing with Ben again—my grandson. This Ben is the son of David and Maggie Niehaus. I hope over the next few years I will make more time to fish with all my grandchildren and get to know them as I did Grandpa Ben.

Bernie fishing with two of his grandchildren, Nicholas and Megan Niehaus, at Kentucky Lake

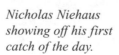

Nicholas Niehaus showing off his first catch of the day.

Bernie fishing with grandson, Ben Niehaus, at Kentucky Lake.

"I would be remiss if I didn't highlight some key people who helped make our company successful."

70 Years of Memories

From *Niehaus News*, April, 2003

In celebrating our 70th anniversary this year, I would be remiss if I didn't highlight some key people who helped make our company successful. They are still living and enjoying their retirement.

Tom Chesser 1953 – 1997

Tom was working for our company when I was in high school. He taught me to drive the truck, load and unload lumber and several other things I will not mention in this article. In 1962, Tom was named the first manager of our Cash-Away Lumber store. In 1984 he became manager of WBM and continued to buy the lumber until his retirement in 1996. Tom was a good manager of the men and really contributed to our success in the growth years.

Horace "Red" Anderson 1955 – 1985

Red, as we all called him, was a superb craftsman. He was the manager of our mill from 1955 to 1970. He could literally make anything you could draw—from cabinets to special order doors, windows, and molding. In 1970 we closed our mill and opened our new WBM Component Plant on Elkhorn Road. He was the first manager and he helped set up our door plant. Red's ability to run the mill operation and fabrication plant helped in making our door plant into the largest in the Tri-state.

Don Burdsall 1972 – 1988

After we enlarged our retail store in the sixties, we needed a good store manager and Don fit the position. Don had been the manager of the A & P Grocery Store so he had great experience with people. Don knew many people in the community and he was a real asset in bringing us new business.

Bob Costello 1970 – 2000

Bob took over our Niehaus Kitchen Department in 1970 and really made a name for himself as a top kitchen designer. He was a real artist and drew renderings of his kitchens, which would really sell the customer. Bob also helped us start our wholesale kitchen division in the early days of WBM.

John Coulup 1978 – 1990

John came to us at just the right time. Mrs. Niehaus was getting ready to retire, and John was a friend of our family and someone we all trusted to take over the check writing and financial part of our company. Also during John's tenure, he helped convert our accounting system from old ledger books to the computer. John was a real asset to our company during the growth years.

Don Burdsall and Tom Chesser with Bernie's
son, Butch Niehaus. Photo taken in 1986.

Bob Costello, Manager of the Kitchen Department and kitchen designer from 1970 to 2000.

Red Anderson, Mill Manager, 1955 to 1985.

John Coulup, Office Manager from 1978 to 1990.

Chapter 2
The Growth Years

- *Michigan State*
- *Cash-Away Lumber*
- *Advertising and Marketing*
- *Customer Service*
- *My Three Sons*
- *Our Family Picnic*
- *The Miracle Begins With You*
- *The Real Recipients*
- *Our 70th Anniversary*

"So much has changed over the past 40 years that it is hard to imagine."

Michigan State

From *Niehaus News*, July, 1999

Forty years ago last month, in June of 1959, I graduated from Michigan State University, and it was at that time I started my career in the lumber business. So much has changed over the past 40 years that it is hard to imagine now. Clayton Miller, the first employee my father and grandfather hired, was still making kitchen cabinets, windows, and doors on his workbench. At that time we were still filling carry-in containers with turpentine and linseed oil from 55-gallon drums. Many kinds of nails still came in the old wooden kegs. Most of our freight came in by rail cars. We were located right next to the New York Central Freight Station and lumber was unloaded by hand from boxcars from the west coast. All of these things have changed—and for the better.

Several of my friends who graduated from Michigan State went to work for a new Cash & Carry Lumber Company in Michigan by the name of Wickes. After visiting these yards, I decided to bring the Cash & Carry concept to Vincennes. In 1961 we opened Niehaus Cash-Away, the first Cash &

Carry yard in the tri-state area. Needless to say, the idea was a fantastic success. In just a few years we grew from the smallest of the five lumberyards in Vincennes to the largest.

By 1969 we had really outgrown our Main Street location. Mrs. Niehaus purchased some land for us right off the Old Decker Road on Elkhorn Road and the railroad tracks. In 1970 we opened WBM—Wholesale Building Materials. At this new location we built roof trusses and pre-hung door units. Also, with our new rail siding we unloaded large flat cars of lumber and building materials. Big Buck Lumber Company in Robinson became our first wholesale customer.

Over the next 30 years, 1969 – 1999, WBM has grown to be one of the largest building material distributors in the tri-state. Now with cabinet showrooms in St. Louis, Nashville, and Collinsville, WBM now distributes Aristokraft cabinets in 5 states.

After the acquisition of Big Buck Lumber in Robinson and Terre Haute, the number of employees has grown from 11 in 1959 to 205. Without a doubt it is to those valuable employees over the years, that I contribute our success.

Wholesale Building Materials, located at 100 Elkhorn Road in Vincennes, Indiana. The business sits on a 60 acre site. It serves as the distribution center for Aristokraft cabinetry, Trus Joist MacMillian engineered lumber, the Therma Tru door mill, a counter top manufacturing plant, and many building material products.

Clayton Miller, our first employee, moved to WBM in 1980 to our new pre-hung door plant.

The 1959 Michigan State Construction Technology class on a field trip visiting a lumberyard in Michigan.

Trusses from our new truss plant which we started in 1960 in our mill building at the Main Street location. These trusses were for the Doll Motel on South 41.

"..and the customers came with their trucks and cash."

Cash-Away Lumber

From *Niehaus News*, June, 2003

In reminiscing about our 70 years, the sixties had to be our biggest growth period percentage-wise. Remembering the Wick's Cash & Carry yards that I had seen and visited while at Michigan State, I decided it was time for me to try their new method of selling.

So in 1961 an old building behind our lumberyard on Vigo Street became available. It was the old Recola Bottling Works, an early Vincennes soft drink company owned by the Recker family. We bought the building and opened up Cash-Away Lumber Company—Southern Indiana's first Cash & Carry lumber yard. Tom Chesser was named the manager of our new Cash-Away Lumber. Tom remained with our company for over 38 years until he retired in 1997.

In those days a conventional lumberyard used a typical selling margin of about 30%. A cash & carry yard used an average of 15% margin. Therefore our prices were considerably lower than our competitors. This was possible because two of the greatest expenses of a lumberyard were delivery and carrying the charge accounts. When I was in high school I would make 10 to 15 deliveries a day with the pickup truck. I remember delivering a quart of paint every summer to an elderly lady so she could paint her porch. By eliminating the free delivery expense and by getting cash, our new Cash-Away could be profitable on these lower margins.

One of our good contractors, Jack Sievers, came in the yard one day and told us the other lumber dealers were saying, "That young Niehaus kid is going to go broke." Needless to say, we didn't go broke.

The advertising in those days for a cash & carry yard was a single four-page flyer with prices only—no pictures. Gil Kramer of Kramac Printing printed as many as 50 thousand of these flyers at a time. We circulated the flyers within a 40 mile radius of Vincennes and the customers came with their trucks and cash.

Cash-Away Lumber on Vigo Street was a huge success and by 1964 was out-growing its small office. So we decided to combine our two yards, Niehaus Lumber and Cash-Away, and call it Niehaus Cash-Away.

Tom Chesser—the first manager of our Cash-Away Lumber business.

1962. Mrs. Naomi Niehaus checking out the cash register at the end of the business day.

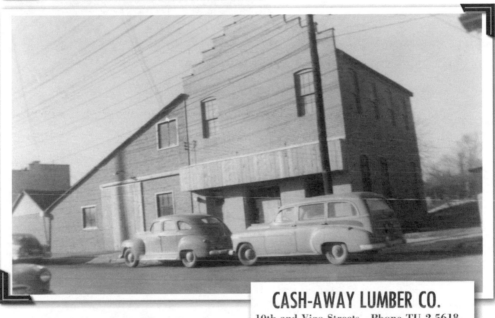

The old Recola Bottling Company, owned by the Recker family and later purchased by Robert Meeks for a sheet metal business. We then purchased the property to become the first cash and carry lumber business in the area.

First flyer printed by Kramac Printing.

"Several of our promotions were not very successful — two were real duds — marbles and panty hose."

Advertising and Marketing

From *Niehaus News*, August, 2003

Over the last 40 years the most exciting and fun part of our business was the advertising and marketing. In my senior year at Michigan State, I had an excellent professor in marketing, and also in advertising. In my advertising course, I worked out ads for our lumber company and sent them back to the Vincennes newspaper. I think my professor liked this actual experience, because I got an "A" in the course.

During the early sixties, we used a cartoon-like character in our newspaper ads called "Bill Ding" (Building). I had a likeness of the Bill Ding character built out of plywood. He had a box-like body, round head with cutouts for the armholes, eyes and mouth. We would use the Bill Ding suit for special promotions and parades. One 4th of July Parade, I wore the bright yellow box and marched down Main St. and back down Hart St. It was 90 degrees and before the parade ended, I thought I was going to have a heart attack. Later as my kids grew up, they would put the suit on and parade up and down in front of our store to draw traffic.

Over the years, we have used many promotions. One year for a Labor Day Sale, we gave one melon with each $10.00 purchase. We gave away two truck-loads of watermelons. For another promotion we bought 300 spruce saplings for a "Spruce Up Your Home Sale." We bought 500 hockey sticks at a bargain price one year, and our timing was perfect with a real cold weekend.

We had sky divers land in our parking lot for a promotion—but we never got many people in the store. Several of our promotions were not very successful—two were real duds—marbles and panty hose. The kids were supposed to bring their parents in and get a handful of marbles. The kids came in, but not the parents. Panty hose was definitely a bust—they just didn't go in a lumberyard.

However, many of our promotions did work and they certainly brought in store traffic. But another real benefit of all these promotions was it made our store a fun place to work.

We have had many successful promotions over the years. Shown here are the NASCAR model, the chainsaw sculptor artist, and a live band playing during our grand opening.

The "Bill Ding" character used in our advertising, parades, and promotions to identify our store.

One of the cutest promotions was a pumpkin coloring contest for the children. We supplied the pumpkins and markers and the children came in and designed their pumpkins. Prizes were awarded in several categories and everyone had fun.

"Good customer service is when you care about your customers' project or their needs."

Customer Service

From *Niehaus News*, February, 2000

Customer service is the life blood of any company. A customer today can buy from a discount store, a warehouse store, and now the internet. Only good customer service will make the difference regarding where a customer buys.

T. Scott Gross, author of the book *Positively Outrageous Service*, explains that this is service that makes your customer say "WOW." In his book, he gives many examples of companies and employees who have performed this kind of service and he recommends that P.O.S. awards be set up for employees that perform this kind of Positively Outrageous Service.

Just this last weekend, Patty and I decided to go to our cabin on Kentucky Lake. We got down there a few minutes before 5:00 Friday evening and discovered that we had no heat and it was ice cold. Upon checking, we found that we were out of propane fuel. The gas company had forgotten to fill our tank. I called the gas company; my mood not a very good one. A very nice lady named Theresa answered the phone. I explained our plight. She explained that it was after 5:00 and she was the only one there—but she would get on the radio and see if she could catch a driver. Forty minutes later a driver showed up and filled our tank and turned the heat on. Later we found out the driver was the manager. Both he and Theresa deserve a P.O.S. award—that's Positively Outrageous Service!

Good everyday customer service does not have to always be Positively Outrageous. Good customer service is when you care about your customers' project or their needs. It's when you smile or call your customer by name and it's when you say "thank you" in a way the customer really knows you mean it.

It is our goal to set ourselves apart from all the others by offering the very best customer service possible.

For the last few years, we have offered our customers free popcorn to enjoy while they shop. We have also offered our contractors free ice and iced tea during the hot summer months, coffee in the winter, and on some days, free donuts.

We offer our do-it-your-self customer, as well as the professional, advice and assistance with product choices for their projects at our three retail stores.

Customer being assisted by our current manager, Phil Wehrman.

The Niehaus News is a monthly publication covering events in the company, as well as the accomplishments of its employees. Over 4,000 copies are mailed each month to our contractors, customers, friends, vendors and employees.

Roofing being delivered to the rooftop for our customer.

"I am not retiring—I'm having too much fun watching this family business grow."

My Three Sons

From *Niehaus News*, March, 2000

It seems like just yesterday when my mother came to me in the office one day and said, "Bernie, I think you should be the President of this company now." She had been running the company since my father's death. It was 40 years ago that my mother entrusted the company to me. Now it's time for the leadership to change again.

My three sons are ready to take over this leadership role. In grade school they dusted paint cans and swept the floors. In high school they loaded lumber and drove the trucks. After college, they assumed manager positions and have made many changes in the last ten years. Our sales growth has doubled twice in this time period.

It has been very rewarding to work with my three sons and see the enthusiasm and energy I had 40 years ago. In just a few years I hope I will be watching the fifth generation start to dust paint cans.

Not only have Patty and I been blessed with three fine sons, but also with two great daughters. They are now officially part of the Niehaus Family

Business as stockholders and new Directors of the corporation. My oldest daughter, Anne, is a school teacher in Hickory, N.C. She and Bob have four children. Catherine, my youngest daughter, is a National Certified Counselor in Peoria, IL. She and her husband Steve have two children and are expecting a third. My daughters will be contributing to the business from the sidelines.

I am not retiring—I'm having too much fun watching this family business grow, so I will remain Chairman and C.E.O. However, Patty and I will be taking more time off to be with and visit our 14 grandchildren with three more on the way.

Eric, David and Butch Niehaus looking over a remodeling project at Wholesale Building Materials.

Bernie Niehaus with his three sons: David Niehaus, Vice-President of Sales, Butch Niehaus, President, and Eric Niehaus, Vice-President of Operations.

My three sons—and my two daughters. David, Butch, Eric, Catherine and Anne—shown with their mother, Patty, and me.

"These special people read like the Who's Who in the Niehaus Lumber family history."

Our Family Picnic

From *Niehaus News*, October, 1999

This year's Niehaus Family Picnic, our 23rd, was the largest ever. Over 400 persons attended, representing all seven of our locations. I was especially pleased that we had such a nice turnout from our newest family members— Big Buck in Robinson and Terre Haute.

The children all seemed to have a real good time with the Velcro Olympics, Air Moonwalk, Mini Indy and the Space Laser. These were the new play attractions this year.

The Service Awards, Sales Awards, and Safe Driving Awards were all given out, but the highlight of the awards were the Extra Mile Awards. This year's Extra Mile awards were given to all our locations. The award is a pure gold Austrian Ducat mounted in a gold bezel suspended on a gold chain. This award has been given out for the last 20 years at our company picnics. These special people read like the Who's Who in the Niehaus Lumber family history.

It has been very rewarding to see the growth of the past recipients over the years. Many of the Extra Mile award winners started at entry-level jobs and now they are in managerial positions. A few of these people—like Jean Fox, now our Niehaus Office Manager, Phil Wehrman, our Niehaus Store Manager, Sherry Cummins, our Advertising Manager, and Kim Smith, our Lumber and Commodities Buyer—are now key persons in our company.

Extra Mile Awards

1979	Roy Roach
1980	Doug Flickner
1981	Octave Quinett
1982	Jack Goldman, Don Burdsall
1983	Lawrence Lemons, Kim Smith
1984	Mike Worland, Tim Wilson
1985	Mike McCarter, Mary K. Edgin
1986	John Coulup, Debi Moyes
1987	Paul Kopp, Sherry Cummins
1988	Stan Eck, Troy Eubank
1989	Andrea Blocker, Danny Harrington
1990	Joey Steinwachs, Kathy McCreary
1991	Judy Detty, Dave Clevy
1992	Phil Wehrman, Alan Wagner
1993	Jerry Burch, Mike Leech
1994	Mike Taylor, Larry Kellams
1995	Jean Fox, Kim Sims
1996	Mike Cavender, Eric Feagley
1997	Sharon English, Bill Hageman
1998	Doug Mikiska, Clete Yochum, Deb Harrison
1999	Don Pea, Todd Donovan, Larry McCoy, Evelyn Bittner, Dean Franz
2000	Lisa Ridgeway, Lynn McCleave, Ralph Ross, Matt Schick, Bill Egbert, Kim Terry
2001	Tracy Hall, Dan Martens, Gary Chillingworth, Brian Childs
2002	Tim Boone, Keith Fox, Rebecca Taylor, Shannon Grantham, Susan Sanders
2003	Stephanie Zachary, Lisa Litherland, Al Lepsi, Tim Murray, Mary Beth Robinson

The Niehaus Companies Family Picnic is an annual event that brings the employees from all six companies and their families together for an evening of fun and fellowship.

The annual picnic is planned to entertain the children with rides, games, and prizes as well as a great dinner and an awards program and prizes for the employees.

" . . . you will see a miracle and so will we."

The Miracle Begins With You

From *Niehaus News*, July, 2000

Several years ago Dr. Phillip Summers, President of Vincennes University, in his opening remarks to the freshman class, used the theme, "The Miracle Begins With You." The idea he presented was that whatever effort they put into college would equate later to what they would get out of life. This same theme holds true for all of us as we go through life. That extra effort we put into our family relations, our community, and our job will equate to success in our life.

Steven Covey, in his #1 best selling book, *The 7 Habits Of Highly Effective People,* lists "Be proactive" as habit number one. He says, "…it means that as human beings we are responsible for our own lives. We have the initiative and the responsibility to make things happen."

This September at our annual company/family picnic, we will again be awarding the prestigious "Extra Mile" awards. These awards are given to the people who make things happen. Throughout the years many of these employees are now managers in our company. Several of them have gone on to a very successful career in another business.

Harvey MacKay, in his article "Going The Extra Mile Pays Off" listed guidelines to life and business by an anonymous author:

DO MORE THAN

Do more than exist; Live!
Do more than hear; Listen!
Do more than agree; Cooperate!
Do more than talk; Communicate!
Do more than spend; Invest!
Do more than think; Create!
Do more than work; Excel!
Do more than share; Give!
Do more than consider; Commit!

So at the beginning of this 21st Century, set your goals now to 'do more than' and put extra effort into your family relations, your community, your job, and "Let the Miracle Begin With You." You will see a miracle and so will we.

Bernie takes time out to read to a Flaget Elementary School class. Assisting him is grand-daughter, Mallory Niehaus.

In The Seven Habits of Highly Effective People, *author Stephen R. Covey reveals a step-by-step pathway for living with fairness, integrity, honesty, and human dignity—principles that give us the security to adapt to change, and the wisdom and power to take advantage of the opportunities that change creates.*

January 20, 2004—Bernie and Dr. Summers look over the first proof of this book to be published in the next couple of months.

"The real recipients of this award should be our many valuable employees...both current and retired."

The Real Recipients

From *Niehaus News*, May, 2001

Last week Patty and I drove up to Indianapolis to receive the very prestigious Half-Century Award from the state. I really wish my Grandfather, Dad and Mother could have been there. They would have been very proud to see the business that they started has now lasted over 68 years. 2003 will be our 70th Anniversary.

The real recipients of this award should be our many valuable employees we have had over these years—both current and retired. The following list shows that many of our current employees have been with us for a number of years. The names represented are those who have been with our company for 5 years or more.

Don Mendenhall	35 years	Roy Roach	30 years
Ken Doades	29 years	Kim Smith	28 years
Sherry Cummins	26 years	Carl Hensley	26 years
Jerry Burch	26 years	Larry McCoy	26 years
Debi Moyes	25 years	Larry Kellams	25 years

Michael Welsh	24 years	Phil Wehrman	25 years
Clete Yochum	24 years	Mark Ashcraft	22 years
Mike Worland	21 years	Paul Kopp	20 years
Cathy Yochum	19 years	Lynn McCleave	19 years
Keith Fox	18 years	Kathy McCreary	18 years
Dan Harrington	17 years	Ginger Welton	17 years
Jean Fox	16 years	Betty Tuttle	16 years
Judy Detty	16 years	Bill Stevens	15 years
Becky Taylor	13 years	Mike Cavender	12 years
Doug Mikiska	12 years	Eric Feagley	10 years
Dean Franz	10 years	Kevin Grostefon	9 years
Helen Smith	9 years	Steve McNew	8 years
Brad Snider	8 years	Michael Jones	8 years
Paul Martin	8 years	Tim Morris	8 years
Dale Nash	8 years	Steve Taylor	8 years
Deborah Dunn	8 years	Sue Fox	7 years
Dan Martens	7 years	Todd Donovan	7 years
John Harrison	7 years	Lisa Ridgeway	7 years
Steve Gerdemann	7 years	Juanita Lamparter	7 years
Lisa Litherland	6 years	Wayne Sullivan	6 years
Dennis Bilskie	6 years	Kyle Blubaum	6 years
Shawn Brothers	6 years	Candy Walls	6 years
Ron Gaines	6 years	Connie Lockhart	6 years
Fred Robinson	6 years	Susan Sanders	6 years
Brian Smith	6 years	Randy Stephens	6 years
George Unsworth	6 years	Don Kirby	6 years
Martha Olker	6 years	Steve Rooker	6 years
Kim Terry	6 years	Phil Cutshall	5 years
Rick Daniel	5 years	John Adams	5 years
Rick Henry	5 Years	Stephen Lanning	5 Years
Shannon Grantham	5 years	Gary Chillingworth	5 years
Alan Smith	5 years	Kevin Toole	5 years
Doug Vantlin	5 years	Bill Egbert	5 years
Dominic Pendino	5 years	Joy Whiteside	5 years
Al Lepsi	5 years	Tim Boone	5 years
William Wait	5 years		

Our retirees are: Tom Chesser, Red Anderson, John Coulup, Bob Costello, Don Burdsall, Bob Frisz, Bernice Jordon, Mary K. Edgin, Sharon English and Betty Neal. In addition, there are several long-time employees who have since passed away.

These wonderful people have dedicated the major part of their lives to this company. It is with these people that we would like to share this very special award.

Kim Smith, Commodities Buyer, being presented a plaque honoring his 25th year with our company by Bernie Niehaus and Butch Niehaus.

Patty Niehaus, Bernie Niehaus, and Mayor Mooney at the Half-Century Awards banquet where Niehaus Companies was presented a prestigious award.

"My grandpa told the story about sprinkling sawdust around to make it look like they were busy."

Our 70th Anniversary

From *Niehaus News*, February, 2003

This year, 2003, marks the 70th year for Niehaus Lumber. All 70 years have been at the same location—11th & Main Streets. Later on this year we will publish a special edition of the Niehaus News with pictures and stories of the past 70 years.

In 1933, right in the middle of the Depression, my father (Francis) and my grandfather (Ben) opened up Niehaus Planing Mill at 11th and Main Streets where our new Niehaus Home Center is today. Business was slow in those days and my grandfather told the story about sprinkling sawdust and shavings around on the floor to make it look like they were busy.

During the Depression years and World War II in the early 1940's, it was very hard to get lumber. My grandpa would go on the mill trips to buy the lumber for us. I went on several of these trips with him. This was my first introduction to the lumber business.

They needed this lumber for our mill shop where they made kitchen cabinets, door frames and windows—all beginning with rough lumber. Francis would order truck loads of roofing, cement and building materials for resale. This became the most successful part of the business, as the need for custom millwork began to fade away.

In November of 1944, at the age of 36, my father died of tuberculosis. His untimely death left a void in the retail lumber business. To fill the void, Naomi Niehaus, the young widow and mother of two small children, came to work in the office to carry on Francis' position. I was just seven and my sister Sondra was six years old. My mother had a difficult task ahead. Being a woman in the lumber business was a very rare circumstance in those days. With a firm purpose and unfaltering determination, the business grew.

Highlights of our 70 years

1933   Ben and Francis Niehaus start Niehaus Planing Mill.

1938   Francis adds retail lumber and roofing.

1944   Francis dies of tuberculosis.

1945   Ben Niehaus retires, Naomi Niehaus becomes president

1959   Bernie Niehaus graduates from Michigan State University and joins family business.

1961   Cash-Away Lumber opens on Vigo Street.

1964   Niehaus Cash-Away opens new self-service store.

1970   WBM purchases land on Elkhorn Road. Opens component plant and distribution center.

1987   Butch Niehaus joins family business.

1989   David Niehaus joins family business.

1992   Eric Niehaus joins family business.

1992   Center Hardware opens, burns down in 1993.

1995   Top Shop (counter top manufacturer) opens.

1996   New Niehaus Home Center Super Store opens.

1996   WBM opens new showroom in St. Louis.

1997   New Rental Center opens at Niehaus.

1998   WBM opens new showroom in Nashville.

1999   Niehaus Companies purchases two Big Buck stores in Terre Haute and Robinson.

2000   Butch Niehaus elected President of Niehaus Companies, Inc.

2001   Karran USA—National importer and distributor of sinks.

NIEHAUS
Companies

• Vincennes, IN

• Robinson, IL
• Terre Haute, IN

• Vincennes, IN

• Vincennes, IN
• St. Louis, MO
• Nashville, TN

• Vincennes, IN

Niehaus Cash-Away in the early 60's.

Niehaus Home Center - after complete renovation in 1996.

Wholesale Building Materials, located on Elkhorn Road in Vincennes, Indiana.

Chapter 3
My Family

"At Kentucky Lake, we really get to spend some quality time with our grandchildren."

A Full House

From *Niehaus News*, Sept/Oct, 2000

I thought that when I built our home back in 1978, with five children, six bedrooms would be ample. Everybody said, "You built too big of a house; the children will leave and you will have a big empty house." WRONG! With 17 grandchildren, plus our five children and their spouses, we have 29 to make a really FULL HOUSE.

With Nana's free babysitting service, the house is a beehive of activity. Papaw loves to play with the grandchildren and he has all kind of games for them; the chopper machine, the bad egg shoot, the rollers, and many, many more, but his favorite is nibbling on ears.

Our lake house at Kentucky Lake has become the most popular place for our grandchildren. It, too, is a FULL HOUSE, and will need expanding. Twenty six of us were there this past 4th of July and it has only four bedrooms.

At Kentucky Lake, we really get to spend some quality time with our grandchildren. They love to ride the wave-runner and the pontoon boat—but, their favorite thing to do is go to Gala Gala Island in Nana's little paddleboat. They bury hidden treasure for the next week's group to find.

These 17 grandchildren are certainly making life more interesting. My birthday is next month and I have asked for the new "Harry Potter" book. I want to be ready for this next generation of our Niehaus family.

Family is a tremendous thing and it should be everyone's number one priority.

At First There Were Five…David, Catherine, Eric, Anne, and Butch Niehaus.

Off to Gala Gala Island in Nana's Paddle Boat
Nicholas Niehaus, Nana, Ben Niehaus, Megan Niehaus, and Johnie Lawless.

Now, There Are More…Charlie Niehaus, Abby Niehaus, Katie Niehaus, Molly Niehaus, Mickey Lawless, Megan Niehaus, Natalie Niehaus, Johnie Lawless, Jackson Niehaus, Kevin Pratt, Ben Niehaus, Bailey Niehaus, Emily Niehaus, Nicholas Niehaus, Alec Pratt, Jensen Lawless, Julia Pratt, Mallory Niehaus, and Brennan Pratt.

*Steve and Jensen Lawless
off on the wave-runner.*

*Loaded for a pontoon
boat ride.*

*First adventure on Kentucky
Lake in our houseboat.*

"...thank God for all those wonderful things we have here in America."

Thanksgiving—A Time for Family

From *Niehaus News*, November, 2001

Now as Thanksgiving grows near and we look back on the tragic events of September 11, let us ask God's blessing for all those families during this special time. Let us also be thankful that we can share this Thanksgiving with all of our families.

When planning for our family Thanksgiving, we thought that our big dining room table, which seats 14, would be ample. Now we have added our kitchen table for eight and two more card tables to accommodate our family of 30.

It has been a tradition for many years that I get up at 4:00 A.M. and put the big bird in the oven. This is why I have earned the nickname of "turkey boy." Patty has set a rule that the turkey must be done by 11:00 so she can use the juices for the dressing.

Another tradition the last 12 years is that Butch's wife, Tina, brings the dumplings and they are delicious. Tina's family raises chickens and they save the old hens to give the dumplings that special flavor. Several years ago when our oldest daughter Anne was living in Chicago, she wanted to make dumplings like Tina's so she asked the butcher for an old hen—I think he thought she was crazy.

After the meal and the dishes are done, some of us watch the football games and many of our family take a walk around beautiful Lakewood Park. Later in the day, after the naps and a few card games, we get out the leftovers and enjoy the meal again.

As you prepare for and enjoy your time with your family, thank God for all those wonderful things we have here in America.

God Bless America! Happy Thanksgiving.

Teresa Niehaus, Anne Niehaus, David Niehaus, and Butch Niehaus help with the preparation of Thanksgiving dinner.

Butch sneaks a nap after Thanksgiving dinner.

Some of the children take a walk in the woods at Papa and Nana's house.

"I hope that your family will start a Christmas tradition this year . . ."

Christmas Memories

From *Niehaus News*, Dec/Jan, 2001

My wife truly loves the Christmas Season. Every room is decorated in our home with a special theme for each room. Nativity scenes from all over the world in one room, another is Santa's, and one in her prized Dickens Village.

One of the traditions she started years ago to kick off the Christmas season was by celebrating the Feast of Saint Nicholas on December 6th. He is the Patron Saint of Children.

This tradition started many years ago in Holland with Sinter Klaas dressed as a medieval Bishop. His assistant was a little Moorish man called Zwart Piet (Black Peter). On St. Nicholas Eve, Sinter Klaas and Zwart Piet delivered gifts to the children. The kids would leave their wooden shoes outside their bedroom door. This is thought to be where the tradition of hanging stockings began. Sinter Klaas would leave gifts for the good children and Zwart Piet would leave a lump of coal or switches for the bad kids.

To carry on this tradition over the years, usually the father dressed up as

Sinter Klaas and the eldest son as Zwart Piet.

You guessed it. Yours truly dressed up as Sinter Klaas, and Butch, our oldest son, dressed as Zwart Piet (Black Peter). I think he really enjoyed giving Eric (our youngest son) the switches and lumps of coal.

Giving the children a little gift on St. Nicholas really starts off the Christmas Season in our family and has been a tradition that Patty has kept up with the grandchildren.

I hope that your family will start a Christmas tradition this year whether it will be an Advent Wreath, celebration of St. Nicholas Feast, or simply spending more time with your family during this Holy Season—the time that we celebrate the coming of our Saviour, Jesus Christ.

I wish you and your families a very Blessed and Holy Christmas.

From only five children at Christmas—to 19.

Original five Niehaus children portraying Nativity scene.

All 19 grandchildren participating in Nativity scene.

Christmas, 1972.
Anne, Eric, David,
Butch, and Catherine.

Christmas, 2001.
Nana and Papa and
the grandchildren.

Dr. Charlie Vieck joins the Christmas sing-a-long at a party at our house.

"Each and everyone of us has the ability to leave a legacy."

Leaving a Legacy

From *Niehaus News*, July, 2001

On June 28th, the 21st Annual Indiana Lumber Dealers Association Golf Outing was held here at our Elk's Country Club. This has been an annual event here since I was President of the Association in 1980. The Lumber Dealers throughout the state have many compliments every year about our course and they love to come here.

This year I was presented a surprise award by our Association Executive, Ray Moistner. The award was a beautiful framed lithograph with the poem, "Leaving A Legacy." Ray spoke highly of our company and complimented my three sons who are in the business with me.

This family business has been a wonderful legacy. In just 18 months we will be celebrating our 70th Anniversary since my grandfather and father started the business in 1933. My mother, Mrs. Naomi Niehaus, is still living and serves on the Board of Directors, along with my two daughters, Anne Niehaus Pratt, and Catherine Niehaus Lawless.

We hope this legacy will live on for many years to come. The fifth generation (our 17 grandchildren) is getting close to starting work—dusting paint cans as I did and my children did in grade school many years ago.

Leaving a legacy can mean much more than leaving a business or an estate. Each and every one of us has the ability to leave a legacy. One with artistic ability can leave a legacy in paintings, carvings, or many other art forms. A good writer can leave a legacy in a book, poem, or an essay. Volunteering is also a good way to leave a legacy. The local YMCA, Senior Center, or churches are all in need of good volunteers. One might want to leave a legacy for a loved one. This can be done by endowing a need for your church in his or her name or also by endowing a scholarship to a school.

Leaving a legacy is a human trait in all of us. This past June was Leave a Legacy Month. It is a chance for us to give something to the future.

1993. Bernie and Mallory Niehaus check out the Pink Panther during the Grand Opening celebration for Center Hardware.

Mrs. Naomi Niehaus observes her 90th Birthday at a family celebration in Bernie's home.

1978. The Suburban Legacy. Patty and children; David, Eric, Catherine, Anne, and Butch, in front of the first of five Suburbans that followed over the years.

Vincennes University Legacy. All five Niehaus children attended V.U. for two years and then moved on to colleges of their choice.

"...Papaw and Nana enjoyed the cruise as much as the boys."

Memories of Our Disney Cruise

From *Niehaus News*, June, 2002

Last month, Patty and I decided to take two of our grandchildren on the famous Disney Cruise—a child's ultimate vacation. Alec, son of Anne and Bob Pratt, and Nicholas, son of Butch and Tina Niehaus, were the two lucky grandchildren this year. They were the perfect age for the trip. Alec is seven and never meets a stranger, and Nicholas is six, and is quiet and shy.

We arrived at the Big Boat about 2:00 on Sunday. After having lunch on a beautiful upper deck, we headed for the sunny pool. There were three pools on this boat. The boys picked the Mickey Mouse Pool because it had a huge deck high enclosed water slide. Butch had told me to be sure and keep an eye on the boys. Well, after about five minutes in Mickey Mouse Pool, I lost them. It's amazing, in a pool of all six- and seven-year-old kids with wet heads, how much they look the same.

After finding the boys, we all got dressed and got ready for the first night's events. There was a big Sail-Away party at 5 P.M when the boat left the dock. A live band on the upper deck provided the entertainment. The boys danced with all the Disney characters to the songs of YMCA, Celebration, and The Chicken Dance. Nana and Papa had a great time also—the boat was rocking and rolling.

The huge eleven-deck boat had two theaters. The first night we went to a Disney produced, live show—"Hercules the Musical." Wow, what a day—the boys went to sleep fast.

When we woke up, we were looking at the Bahamas. After breakfast, we left the ship and walked into Nassau. The first stop was the Straw Market. The boys couldn't understand the bargaining process—they wanted to pay the first price. Patty helped negotiate the prices for them. After a walk around Nassau, we went back to the boat for lunch. The boys wanted to go to Disney's Oceanic Lab, a playroom full of computers, microscopes, and all types of lab equipment. One day the boys made "Flubber," but had to promise not to put it into their brother's or sister's socks. Another lab day they made a rocket ship and a volcano using baking soda. We could hardly get the boys to leave the lab to see the many other things on the boat.

One day the boat docked at Island of Castaway Cave, the dreaded home of Captain Hook. The boys met up with Captain Hook and had their pictures taken with him.

All in all, I think Papa and Nana enjoyed the cruise as much as the boys. It certainly was a great way to spend quality time with two of our grandchildren.

Alec, Nicholas, and Bernie crusin' in style aboard the Disney boat.

Alec and Nicholas meet a
special friend on their
"special trip"
with Nana and Papa.

Bailey and Emily Niehaus
with Snow White.

"God has certainly blessed our marriage and our family."

Our 40th Anniversary

From *Niehaus News*, October, 2002

As I recounted in an earlier "Splinters," Patty and I became engaged on Easter in 1962. I gave her the ring and we attended the Easter Vigil service at Saint Meinrad. This was a very beautiful ceremony, which included the blessing of the water, a procession of all the monks with the live Easter Lamb, and the trumpets sounding the joy of Easter. This truly made our engagement a very memorable occasion.

We were then married on October 13, 1962—40 years ago. Patty and I were married at her parish church, St. Simon's in Washington, Indiana. Father Fred Niehaus, Father Al Niehaus, and Father Pat Foster celebrated the Nuptial Mass. Patty's Uncle Cabby O'Neill gave her away. There were 19 in the wedding party including Patty's four sisters and my sister. It was quite an extravagant affair.

I am still taking quite a ribbing about our honeymoon. There was a national lumber convention in Chicago the week of our honeymoon. So, I thought we could attend that first, before going to New York for our honeymoon. Needless to say, it was something I never lived down.

Our first home was on 1314 Weed Lane and after five years, we quickly outgrew this home with the birth of Anne, Butch, Catherine, and David. So we moved to 1202 Sycamore, where Eric was born. It was 10 years later that we built our new home at Lakewood, where we have lived for the past 25 years.

God has certainly blessed our marriage and our family. He has given us five great children and five wonderful spouses, and they have given us 19 grandchildren who are now the light of our lives.

Over the next several years, we will be kept quite busy in attending First Communions, Confirmations, Graduations, Birthdays, and Weddings. In the next 20 years, this calculates out to be over 100 celebrations of joy and thanksgiving. Thanks be to God.

Our first home on Weed Lane in Vincennes.

Our second home on 12th and Sycamore Streets.

Our current home was built in 1978. It is built on a site that was the home of Lakewood Park, an amusement park in the late 1930's.

We celebrated our 40th Anniversary in Vermont with our two daughters, Catherine and Anne.

Our wedding was held at
St. Simon's Church in Washington,
Indiana. The Nuptial Mass was
celebrated by Father Alfred
Niehaus, Father Fred Niehaus,
and Father Pat Foster.

Patty's Uncle Cabby O'Neill escorts
her down the aisle and gave her away
in the ceremony.

"Take some time away from your everyday routine and relax with your family."

A Florida Tradition

From *Niehaus News*, August, 2003

I just recently returned from a family trip to Florida. It wasn't your average family trip. This one included all five of my children, their spouses, and their 19 children. As my wife, Patty, and I sat on the beach watching the grandchildren play in the waves and build castles in the sand, we couldn't help but remember our past family trips to Florida.

When our children were younger we would load them all up in the family wagon and head south on a 14-hour drive to Florida. Remember, this was well before the invention of the all-important "car TV." The kids would lie in the back across the luggage (who worried about seat belts then?) and read and listen to books recorded on eight-track tapes. I could probably recite the entire story of *Horton Hatches an Egg* to this day. We would spend the days playing in the ocean and building sand castles. I had quite a reputation as a castle builder back then.

I will always cherish the memories of this time together. Away from everyday stress and routines, we just enjoyed being with each other. As I watched my children and grandchildren laugh and play this summer, I thanked God for all our blessings.

Take some time away from your everyday routine and relax with your family. Just think! You're building memories that your children and grand-children will have forever.

Nineteen grandchildren in Destin.

Destin, 2003. Ready with their boogie boards.

1978 St. Pete Beach.

1974 Fort Myers. Patty, David, Anne, Catherine, Butch, and Eric.

"There surely must be a special place in heaven for a grandmother like this."

Nana

From *Niehaus News*, February, 2004

If anyone were looking for the perfect mother and grandmother, my wife, Patty, would have to be the number one candidate. She has her Bachelor and Masters Degree in Education and taught third and fourth grades before we were married. She has since been teaching our five children and now our 19 grandchildren. She will sit and read with each child and has patience beyond belief.

When our five children were growing up, Patty had them all in competitive swimming. That meant she had to get up at 5:00 A.M. and take them to practice before school and then wait for supper until they got out of practice at 7:00 P.M. They also had weekend meets, which incurred high motel and restaurant bills. I griped a lot and gave her a hard time until Anne, our oldest daughter, received a $27,000 scholarship from Northwestern to swim. Scholarships also helped several of our other children. I then realized how important the swimming was for our five children, not only the money, but developing their self-esteem and the ability to get along with others.

Now with our grandchildren, Nana is helping to raise them just as she did with our children. With the patience of "Job", she sits down and plays games with them; she organizes nature hikes, craft work, and picnics. In all the times she is with the kids (and sometimes with all nineteen), I have never heard her raise her voice.

Nana is also an expert in planning trips. For the last four years, two of our grandchildren have been going on special trips each year to "Lego Land" in California and the last two years on the Disney Cruise. They have been going by age:

1st year	Mallory	(Butch & Tina, parents)
	Brennan	(Bob & Anne, parents)
2nd year	Jensen	(Steve & Catherine, parents)
	Julia	(Bob & Anne, parents)
3rd year	Nicholas	(Butch & Tina, parents)
	Alec	(Bob & Anne, parents)
4th year	Bailey	(Eric & Teresa, parents)
	Emily	(David & Maggie, parents)

Nana shops all year for matching outfits to go on their special trip—this really builds excitement for the kids. There surely must be a special place in heaven for a grandmother like this.

Nana creates fun play settings to entertain the grandchildren.

Girls' time out—a special trip for the female grandchildren with Nana.

Nana helps bring out the creativity in the grandchildren with fun projects.

Nana takes the grandchildren on a nature walk.

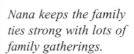

Nana keeps the family ties strong with lots of family gatherings.

Kids and dog go on a fun-inspired trek in the woods, headed up by Nana.

Chapter 4
My Community

- *Rich in History*
- *Giving Back*
- *Trees*
- *Economic Growth—V.U. Technology Building*
- *Our Industry Supports Habitat*
- *Lakewood Park*
- *A Bright Future*
- *Red Skelton—An American Legend*
- *A Dream Come True*

"Several historians have said that the Arch should be in Vincennes, instead of St. Louis."

Rich in History

From *Niehaus News*, September, 2003

My community is certainly rich in history. About a thousand years ago, the mound building Indians inhabited this area. Two large mounds south of town attest to their activities. On the banks of the Wabash was the old Buffalo Trace, which brought the Piankashaw and Shawnee Indians, and later the French fur traders.

In 1778, the British occupied Fort Sackville here. In February of 1779, George Rogers Clark and a volunteer army of French, Indians, and Americans captured the fort from the British. A dramatic turning point in the Revolutionary War—that opened the west for expansion. Several historians have said that the Arch should be in Vincennes instead of St. Louis.

The Indiana Territory was born encompassing the present states of Indiana, Illinois, Michigan, Wisconsin, and part of Minnesota. A new capitol for a new land was established at Vincennes. William Henry Harrison was named Governor of the Indiana Territory and later became the ninth President of the United States.

Governor Harrison was the first Chairman of Vincennes University—founded in 1801. Vincennes became a thriving metropolitan city before the city of Chicago existed. Many people called Vincennes the Williamsburg of the West.

We are fortunate to have so many historical sites in our community that bear evidence of days gone by. These are sites that give area residents and visitors a dramatic view of our rich history. Some of them are:

George Rogers Clark Memorial National Park
Old Cathedral—Indiana's oldest church
Grouseland—Governor Harrison's mansion
Old French House—1806
Indiana Territory Capitol Building—1811
Eli Stout Print Shop
Old State Bank—Indiana's first bank
Ft. Knox Site II

Our community leaders have worked hard over the years to preserve these treasures. I think we are pretty lucky to have all that Vincennes has to offer and I am glad to call it home.

Grouseland was the home of William Henry Harrison, Governor of the Indiana Territory (1800–1812), and later the ninth President of the United States (1841). This Georgian mansion, called "White House of the West," was built in 1803–1804. This home is next to the Vincennes University campus on the Wabash River.

The Old Cathedral. The foundation of the present St. Francis Xavier Church was laid on March 30, 1826, by Fr. John Leo Champomier. In 1834 the church became the cathedral of the new Diocese of Vincennes.

The Indiana Territorial Capitol Building is a two-story frame structure held together by wooden pegs. Built in 1805 as a tailor shop, this building has been preserved and is considered the oldest major government building in the midwest. It is now open for tours where it is used to interpret early government in the territory.

George Rogers Clark Memorial located on part of the site of Fort Sackville in Vincennes, was completed in 1937.

"I think our community is doing very well at teaching our children the gift of giving."

Giving Back

From *Niehaus News*, June, 2000

Last month our community held its annual Relay For Life — a team event to fight cancer. I am grateful that many of our employees participated in this very worthwhile cause. Several of the Relay teams sold hot dogs and cookies here at our Home Center to earn money. We were certainly honored to help these teams achieve their goals.

In the opening ceremonies of this moving event, over 205 cancer survivors either walked or were pushed around the initial lap. The 139 teams participating applauded as the survivors made their way to the track.

The most emotional part of the festivities was at 9:00 P.M. when over 2,500 luminaries were lit to honor those who had lost the battle to cancer or to honor a cancer survivor. During a solemn ceremony, the name of each person being remembered or honored was read.

This year this spectacular community event raised over $250,000, one of the largest totals raised for a community of this size. The organizers, the committees, the team captains, and all who participated, are certainly to be congratulated on a tremendous success.

I have heard so many times that we need to teach our future generations the gift of giving back. After witnessing this event, I think our community is doing very well at teaching our children the gift of giving.

Deke Wells, Chairman of Therma-Tru Doors, says: "Giving means we care. Caring means we like to help and helping others is a wonderful and energizing motivator for us all."

I am sure that many of you, just as myself, have found the more you give, the more you receive.

Bernie Niehaus talks with the group participating in the "Bail or Jail" fundraising campaign for the American Cancer Society

Company employees participating in the March of Dimes Walk America.

Back row:
Bob Costello, Clete Yochum, Keith Fox
Middle:
Sherry Cummins, Cathy Yochum, Sharon English, Chris Morine
Front:
Christa Wright, Ginger Welton.

Carolyn Jones Williams with a team of young men, co-sponsored by Niehaus Companies, who were dedicated to raise funds for the Relay for Life.

Our business donates a children's playset to be raffled at the Relay for Life weekend of events.

"Priceless is the word for the beauty of our trees."

Trees

From *Niehaus News*, May, 2000

Last month we celebrated Arbor Day. This is now a special day set aside by our country for all to plant a tree. This year at our Home Center, we gave away over 300 red oak trees. We hope that many of you planted them. Over the years, we have given away thousands of pine and spruce seedlings. Many of our customers have told us how big their trees have grown. Some have even brought in pictures to show us how beautiful they are.

Priceless is the word for the beauty of our trees. In Vincennes we are fortunate to have Gregg Park. In this park, there are well over 25 different species of trees. It is a beautiful place to walk and really capture nature at its best. In the spring, you will see the beautiful white and pink blossoms of the dogwoods and magnificent magnolias. In the fall, the stunning bright yellow leaves of the Ginko trees and the red leaves of the maple. We certainly owe our past city planners a debt of gratitude for their forethought in planning our Gregg Park.

In Joyce Kilmer's poem "Trees," the ending verse is ".....but only God can make a tree." A mystery still unsolved by man is this: God causes the limb of a tree to grow straight out from the trunk for a distance of 40, 50, even up to 60 feet, with no other anchorage than 15 or 18 inches of fibers which lose themselves in the trunk of the tree. I don't believe any human has discovered how to apply this principle in the construction of buildings or bridges.

Trees (wood products) are still a large part of our building material industry. Many environmentalists criticize our use of trees. Wood manufacturing processes consume only 4% of the energy used by all primary industrial raw material manufacturers. Steel and concrete manufacturers consume 56% of this energy. We believe the world should be using more wood, not less, because no other natural resource on earth can match its environmental advantages.

There are well over 25 different species of trees in Gregg Park. Each species has a sign identifying it, making it a learning experience just to walk through the park.

Gregg Park is a beautiful place to walk and really captures nature at its best.

A mystery still unsolved by man is this: God causes the limb of a tree to grow straight out from the trunk for a distance of 40, 50, even up to 60 feet, with no other anchorage than 15 or 18 inches of fiber which lose themselves in the trunk of the tree.

The welcoming entry to Gregg Park offers visitors a clean, green, lush place to walk, jog, picnic, and play.

"Vincennes University can be the heart and support for the economic growth."

Economic Growth—*V.U. Technology Building*

From *Niehaus News*, August, 2000

Last month I was very fortunate to participate in the groundbreaking ceremony for the new Vincennes University Technology Center. This will certainly be a huge catalyst for economic growth in this area. In a recent study, it states that 65% of new jobs will require a two-year degree or technical certification, and 20% a four-year degree with only 15% requiring no degree. For strong economic growth in this area we will need smart, educated employees. Vincennes University can be the heart and support for this economic growth.

The entryway for the new Technology Building, with skylights, will be a showplace for the Midwest. This two-story atrium will organize labs along a "technology gallery" and will display working labs. This will allow visitors to view the activity without interrupting the instructional process.

Some of the programs located in the Technology Building are:
- Computer Integrated Manufacturing
- Architectural Drafting

- Industrial Drafting and Design/CAD
- Machine Trade
- Surveying
- Commercial Art and Design
- Construction Technology
- Electronics
- Laser and Electro-Optics

With this new technology center and all of the new industries surrounding us, I have never seen, in my 40 years in business, such a future for this area as there is today.

The new Technology Building is the center for Computer Integrated Manufacturing, Architectural Drafting, Industrial Drafting and Design/CAD, Machine Trade, Surveying, Commercial Art and Design, Robotics, Electronics, Laser and Electro-Optics.

State-of-the-art machinery offers students hands-on training right in the classroom.

The entryway to the new Technology Building leading up the stairs under the arched glass vaulted ceiling.

The latest in computer equipment has been installed in the new classrooms, offering students top quality training in every aspect of their chosen trade.

Bernie Niehaus and Art Haase, Dean of Technology, look over the equipment in one of the new classrooms in the Technology Building.

"We can certainly be proud of our local homebuilders and our community for taking part in this great work of people helping people."

Our Industry Supports Habitat

From *Niehaus News*, April, 2001

National Association of Home Builders President, Mr. Bruce Smith, and Habitat founder Millard Fuller, joined a group of more than 20 senators working side-by-side in framing up two Habitat homes in our nation's capitol. During a break in construction, Senate Majority Leader, Trent Lott, spoke on the importance of homeownership and building a strong bipartisan effort to combat poverty housing. Senator Lott specifically cited the constructive role the builders continue to play in this very worthwhile cause.

Our local home builders and community have really supported our Habitat house that will be a part of our Parade of Homes this May 5, 6, 12, and 13th.

Several of our industry's suppliers have also joined in supporting Habitat for Humanity. Master Brand Cabinets (parent of Aristokraft) has recently announced their support of Habitat in each of their locations. Dow Chemical, manufacturers of Styrofoam, donates the insulation board for Habitat homes. Whirlpool has committed to providing stoves and refrigerators for every habitat home built in the next five years.

This coming September, the 25th anniversary of Habitat for Humanity International will be celebrated in Indianapolis when a blitz to build 25 homes will be held. Thousands of habitat partners from around the world are expected in Indianapolis. They will come to build, learn, celebrate, and praise God for all that has been accomplished in Habitat's first quarter century.

We can certainly be proud of our local homebuilders and our community in taking part in this great work of people helping people.

If you would like to be a part of this fine program, either donating time or materials, contact Mr. Bill Powell at 812-882-4880.

One of several homes built by Habitat on 11th Street in Vincennes.

Homes built by Habitat for Humanity, providing families the opportunity to own their own home.

Carl Hensley, Niehaus Window and Door Salesman, and Bill Powell, Director of our local Habitat, look over plans for the latest Habitat home.

Summer Scene Lakewood Park, Vincennes, Ind.

"...the old spring, which is still running, is the only remains left of the old Lakewood Park."

Lakewood Park

From *Niehaus News*, October, 2001

In 1971, I purchased 29 beautiful acres of woods on Washington Avenue, not far from the Elks Country Club. Patty and I built our family home in these woods and raised our five children there.

This wooded area was the site of the famous Lakewood Park, and was owned by the Vincennes Street Car Company, which began in 1883. In those days streetcar companies would put an amusement park at the end of the tracks to generate more fares.

No other town of similar size had anything like Lakewood Park. The lake was man-made, large and very deep, being fed by springs. The dam was at least 14 feet high. As many as 50 or 60 boats were at the disposal of those who loved the pastime.

The amusement park also featured a dance pavilion and a band shell where some of the best bands in the country played. The park also had a merry-go-around, a skating rink, and a large figure-eight roller coaster.

In 1998, our 24 acres of woods was sold to Lakewood Development and another 26 adjoining acres from Simpson Nursery was acquired. These 50 acres of woods are being developed into a beautiful new residential community. The new entrance to Lakewood Park features a guardhouse, which was designed from one of the buildings shown on the early 1900's postcard of Lakewood Park.

My oldest son, Butch, and his wife, Tina, built their house next to ours and between us we still have five acres of woods for our grandchildren to play in. One of the places they play is down by the old Lakewood Park. We are very pleased that the old beautiful park will become a great place to live and for children to play.

Summer Scene Lakewood Park, Vincennes, Ind.

Lakewood Park was owned and operated by the Vincennes Street Car Company. The horse-drawn rail system began operating in 1883. It was most active in taking picnickers to Lakewood Park on Sundays.

Marie McQuaid, with her parents, at Lakewood Park, circa 1913.

In Lakewood Park there was a dance pavilion, merry-go-around, and skating rink, as well as a rare figure-eight roller coaster shown on this postcard.

During the spring of 1920, the Vincennes area received a vast amount of rainfall. The water level at the lake reached an all time high and the resulting pressure became so great that the dam broke. In the mid 1920's, Vincennes saw the farm economy fall, the automobile rise, and Lakewood Park close.

"Hundreds of new jobs will be created from these businesses."

A Bright Future

From *Niehaus News*, January, 2002

Several times this past year I have mentioned that in all the 40 plus years that I have been in business, I have never seen such a bright future for this area. By this I mean Knox County and its contiguous counties. From this area we all receive jobs and economic benefit.

At a public meeting several months ago, a Bicknell resident voiced his opinion. He couldn't understand how reducing taxes on Vincennes businesses would help Bicknell. Well, in our company alone, we have over 100 employees from the Knox County area, many from Bicknell, Wheatland, Decker, and Monroe City.

In the past year many new buildings have been built for new business and service providers. This is a very impressive list and I am sure I missed a few:

- V.U. new Technology building
- Leonard Ford
- Y.M.C.A. addition

- Tommy Wolfe Center
- New Social Security building
- Three new restaurants
- F.I.C.—auto parts for Toyota
- Charter Cable
- Renal Center - Office Building - G.S.H.
- Two assisted living facilities
- Two convenience stores
- Block Buster Video and Wet Pets
- Lowe's Home Center
- New Soda Shop

Many of these buildings are still under construction, but will be ready in 2002.

Many people and many groups are responsible for this good fortune. Just to name a few: The Mayor, City Council, County Council, County Commissioners, Chamber of Commerce, K.C.D.C., and our State Representative, John Gregg, and John Frenz. Thanks to all of these people, hundreds and hundreds of new jobs will be created in 2002 from these businesses I have listed.

The YMCA offers many health and fitness programs for both the young and adults. The latest addition to the facility is the Cardio-Exercise Center, with a wide range of exercise equipment.

Tommy Wolfe Center, operated by our local K.C.A.R.C., offers daycare facilities for sick children.

Good Samaritan Hospital first opened its doors in February, 1908, to humble beginnings as a 25-bed facility. It is a well-respected, regional referral medical complex with an operating complement of over 260 beds, serving southwestern Indiana and southeastern Illinois.

Futaba of America Corp., a new plant that opened in our Industrial Park, manufactures parts for the Toyota plant in Princeton.

"The legacy of Red Skelton should be preserved and shared with future generations."

Red Skelton—An American Legend

From *Niehaus News*, July, 2002

From my early childhood, I heard many stories about Red Skelton from my mother, Grandpa Oakes, and from my uncle and aunt, Bert and Viola Fuller. They all grew up together in the north end. My mother remembers Red hanging around the Medicine Shows and the old Pantheon Theater. My uncle Bert Fuller helped tutor Red when he joined the Masonic Lodge.

For many years I remember Red coming back to Vincennes for various activities such as parades, to name his bridge, and perform at Adams Coliseum. One year when Red was riding in the parade down Main Street, he spotted his fifth grade school teacher, Miss Marsh, watching from the side-walk. Red jumped out of his convertible and gave her a big hug and kiss. It was always a gala affair when Red would come back to visit his hometown.

Many people believe the legacy of Red Skelton should be preserved and shared with future generations, not only because his life is a shining example of what is good about America, but also because of the opportunity this offers to all.

Vincennes University is putting plans in motion to construct the Red Skelton Museum and Performing Arts Center. The proposed site for the project will be within a few blocks of Red's birthplace in Vincennes.

Red starred in most entertainment genres—from medicine shows, showboats, the circus, and Vaudeville, to radio, television, and motion pictures during his 84 years. He appeared in 36 feature films, had a successful network radio program for 15 years, and starred in the Red Skelton Show, which ran for 20 years and remains the second longest-running entertainment program ever in network history. He performed for eight U.S. presidents and three Roman Catholic Popes, composed more than 8,000 songs, 64 symphonies, wrote books, and his paintings and drawings remain collectors' treasures.

It really seems fitting to close this 'Splinters' with a poem from Red Skelton.

The time has come to say good night,
    My how time does fly.
We've had a good laugh, perhaps a tear,
    And now we hear good bye.
I really hate to say good night,
    For times like these are few.
I wish you love and happiness
    In everything you do.
The time has come to say good night,
    I hope I've made a friend.
And so we'll say "May God Bless You"
    Until we meet again.

Rendering of the Red Skelton Performing Arts Building that will be constructed in the near future on the Vincennes University Campus.

Where It All Began. *One of the first
places "Big Red" wanted to show
"Little Red," as he called his wife
Georgia, was his birthplace at 111
Lyndale Avenue, Vincennes.*
Photo from June 28, 1970 Sun-Commercial

Red Paints "His" Bridge. *Red
and his wife Georgia visit the Red
Skelton Memorial Bridge. Red
decided to paint the first brush-
full after reading a story in the*
Sun-Commercial *telling of a bid
letting for painting the structure.*

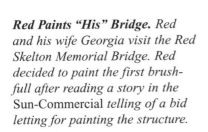

"Our future is bright with this new building."

A Dream Come True

From *Niehaus News*, January, 2003

After graduating from V.U. in 1957, I transferred to Michigan State University and received my B.S. Degree in Building Construction Technology. After graduating in 1959, I came back to Vincennes and had a dream that we would someday have a similar two-year program at V. U. Well, my dream came true. In 1969, Dr. Beckes called me to meet with him and Joe Beach to start a new course in Building Construction Technology. Our first building was the old Wabash Coffee Warehouse across from the Oldsmobile Garage on Second. Street. Next we moved to the side wing of Beliss Gym and then to the Entomology building. Our lab then moved to the old Armory Building next to the Alumni Foundation office. We felt like a stepchild moving from building to building. We dreamed of a new building— a place of our own.

While I was on the Board of Trustees, I kept pushing for a new building and for many years we were in the top five on the priority list. When I resigned from the board, I asked Jim McCormick and Dr. Phillip Summers to keep pushing for our new building. Finally this past year, Phil Rath was able to get our funding approved. This past summer at our Advisory Board meeting, Mr. Ridgway presented the plans for our new building to the committee. What a fantastic job George did. It will have a beautiful glass entryway with a large area where we will be able to showcase our projects and even create a Hall of Fame for our graduates. We will also have conference rooms, and faculty offices—and speaking of faculty, we have the greatest. With all the moving around and poor facilities, they are the ones who held our program together. And we are now the third largest program in the Technology Division.

These faculty members are Brian Lindsey, Rick Ray, Rich Wellage, Mike Hartigan and Bob Weiss. Our graduates also speak well of our faculty and curriculum—our graduates are now some of the best homebuilders in Vincennes, Terre Haute, Indianapolis, and many other cities in the Midwest.

A recent article in *USA Today* told of the three top job opportunities—Information Technology, Health Care, and Construction. V.U. is now ready to train students for the construction market.

Our future is bright with this new building—recruitment will be easy. I challenge our faculty to grow our program to be the largest Technology Division. With the new building, my dream and the dream of many others has finally come true.

Bernie Niehaus, left, former chairman of Vincennes University Board of Trustees, Bryan Blanchard, V.U. President, and George Ridgway of G.S. Ridgway and Associates, following the groundbreaking ceremonies for the new Construction Technologies Facility.

Professors of Construction Technology.
Back: Rich Wellage, Mike Hartigan, Bob Weiss.
Front: Rick Ray and Brian Lindsey.

Vincennes University's new Construction Technology Building was completed in the fall of 2003. General Contractor for the new building was Wolfe Construction Company, Steve Wolfe, President.

Chapter 5
My Church

- *A Very Special Day*

- *The Redwoods*

- *A Roman Holiday*

- *Easter 40 Years Ago*

- *Christmas Memories*

- *Father Niehaus*

- *Saint Meinrad*

" . . . I awkwardly pretended to blow my nose, but was really wiping away tears of pride and joy."

A Very Special Day

From *Niehaus News*, June, 2001

Our family witnessed two very special days during the month of May—the First Communion of our two oldest grandchildren. Mallory Niehaus, daughter of Butch and Tina Niehaus, made her First Communion at St. Vincent's Church here in Vincennes with six other second graders from their parish.

Brennan Pratt, son of Anne and Robert Pratt, made his First Communion at St. Aloysius Catholic Church in Hickory, North Carolina. Sixty-two second graders made their First Communion with Brennan. It was the largest class ever for this parish.

St. Vincent's is a beautiful, small country church with 100 families. St. Aloysius is a large, new, very contemporary church with over 1,000 families.

Even though the churches and the number of people were different, the ceremony and spiritual significance of the day were the same. These precious children were brought to the table of the Lord for the first time.

The little girls wore their white dresses, and veils, and the boys were all dressed in white pants and white shirts. In the homily, Pastors Father Scheller and Father Ed spoke directly to the children, telling them about the importance of this day, and then asked them questions. The pastors also stressed the important role of the parents and grandparents to set a good example.

The big moment finally came as the First Communicants were called up to the altar of the Lord to receive the Body of Christ. The proud parents were clicking away pictures and I awkwardly pretended to blow my nose, but was really wiping away tears of pride and joy.

Yes, these are very special days in the lives of the parents, grandparents, and of course the First Communicants. Our family is looking forward to the next several years. With 17 grandchildren, we have 15 First Communions left to attend.

Butch and Tina's daughter, Mallory's First Communion at St. Vincent Church in Vincennes.

Anne and Bob Pratt's son, Brennan, making his First Communion at St. Aloysius in Hickory, North Carolina.

Bernie and Patty and
daughter, Anne Pratt, at
Julia's First Communion in
Hickory, North Carolina.

Catherine and Steve Lawless
with their daughter, Jensen,
at her First Communion in
Peoria, Illinois, at St.
Philomino.

"You can certainly feel the presence of God and how infinitesimal our life is compared to these 500 to 2000 year old living trees."

The Redwoods

From *Niehaus News*, November, 2000

Early last month, Patty and I attended the wedding of her nephew in San Francisco. After the wedding, we planned a few extra days to head north and see the magnificent redwoods.

Five hours north of San Francisco, near Garberville, we took the world famous scenic drive called The Avenue of the Giants. This is a 31 mile portion of old Highway 101, which winds through over 50,000 acres of redwood groves.

The Avenue of Giants is surrounded by Humboldt Redwood State Park, which has the largest remaining stand of virgin redwoods in the world. In driving along The Avenue of Giants, we saw the Shrine Drive Thru Tree, which is pictured above.

Coast redwoods follow the fog and grow best in less than 2000 feet elevation in areas of heavy winter rains and moderate temperatures. These are the world's tallest living things. Some of them tower above 360 feet. The name "Sequoia Sempervirens" is Latin for "ever living" —an appropriate name for these trees since many are 600 to 1200 years old and some have lived more than 2000 years. At one of our stopping points, we saw a huge redwood that had fallen. You could see the many annual rings. The tree was over 1000 years old. At some of the growth rings a small plaque was attached—one said "1492, the year Columbus discovered America"—another, 1776, for the Revolutionary War, and another for 1860, the Civil War.

Statistics cannot begin to describe the beauty, grandeur, and majestic serenity of these trees. It is a very strange feeling when walking among these very tall giants. You can certainly feel the presence of God and how infinitesimal our life is compared to these 500 to 2000 year old living trees.

Bernie standing at the entrance of the drive-thru tree. September 2000

Patty standing in a magnificent Redwood grove.

The "Chandelier Tree" still lives even with a tunnel cut through its base. The passageway allows most full-sized cars to pass through, but needs to be enlarged every few years as the still-growing tree attempts to close the gap. The Drive Thru Tree is 315 feet tall and 21 feet in diameter.

"When I walked into the church and then up to St. Peter's statue I really felt the presence of God."

A Roman Holiday

From *Niehaus News*, August, 2001

Every other year the USG Company (United States Gypsum) offers an incentive trip to their distributors. This year's trip was to Rome, and USG really outdid themselves. Tim Bixler, Vice-President of Sales, was our host and along with his staff, provided a truly remarkable experience and very enjoyable trip.

Founded in 753 B.C., Rome was the capital of the ancient empire, containing vast lodes of the world's artistic treasures. Few cities have had such an immense impact on the world as Rome. What began as a simple settlement of shepherds grew into a vast empire, with its language, architecture, politics and religion—changing history forever.

Some interesting sights on our tour of Rome were the Coliseum and Roman Forum. The Coliseum is the most stupendous monument of ancient Rome. It was designed to hold 50,000 spectators for gory entertainment. The Roman Forum was the civic heart of austere and stern Rome that flourished in the days of the Republic.

The highlight of our trip to Rome was our visit to St. Peter's Basilica and the Sistine Chapel. When I walked into the church and then up to St. Peter's statue, I really felt the presence of God—remembering the words "upon this rock I will build my church." It was truly an awesome feeling.

The Sistine Chapel closes at 5:00 P.M. so USG arranged a private showing for our group. The chapel was built in 1433 and is still used today for papal elections. The highlights of the Chapel are the frescoes on the ceiling, which Michelangelo spent four grueling years painting.

We had several days of free time built into our schedule, which allowed us to wander the streets of Rome. The Italian people were very friendly and we really enjoyed the sidewalk cafes with pizza and wine for lunch. One of the real benefits of a trip is meeting new friends and acquaintances. Upon leaving the "Eternal City," we all promised to write each other and meet again.

The Tomb of
Pope Innocentius XI

Swiss guard at the gate of St. Peter's.

Patty enjoys the Roman sights.

Bernie in courtyard at St. Peter's.

"Easter is a very Religious Holy Day and a very special day for our family."

Easter 40 Years Ago

From *Niehaus News*, **March, 2002**

Easter is the most important feast day for the Church, and for that matter, all of Christianity, even more important than Christmas. It is because if Christ had not risen from the dead, then there would be no Church, no Christian faith.

A very important thing happened to me 40 years ago on Easter. Patty and I became engaged on Easter 1962. I gave her the ring and we then attended the Easter vigil service at Saint Meinrad. This was a very beautiful ceremony which included the blessing of the water, a procession of all the monks with the live Easter Lamb and the trumpets sounding the joy of Easter. This truly made our engagement a very memorable occasion. We were then married on October 13, 1962.

Easter is truly a family celebration. We all attend the Easter Mass, and of course, the little girls are all dressed up in their new frilly Easter dresses. After Mass, all our children and grandchildren come to our house for a big Easter dinner of ham and all the trimmings.

This past Easter, Patty sat out seventeen Easter baskets from the Easter Bunny for each of the grandchildren—next year it will be nineteen—David and Maggie and Eric and Teresa are each expecting their fourth child.

After dinner, it's time for the annual family egg hunt, a tradition for the last thirty-some years, starting with our children and now the grandchildren. The Easter Bunny hides the eggs in the front yard (guess who the Easter Bunny is) and each year more eggs are needed. Several years ago my mother started to bring plastic eggs with money inside—the bigger children have gotten wise and look for them first.

Yes, Easter is a very Religious Holy Day and a very special day for our family. It all started on that Easter Vigil at Saint Meinrad in 1962, 40 years ago.

Getting ready to say "go" for the Easter egg hunt by Papa Niehaus and Great Grandmother Niehaus.

Grandson Johnny Lawless finds an egg.

Easter dinner in the dining room at Bernie and Patty's.

*Grandchildren in the kitchen being watched by
Anne Pratt and Aunt Barbara.*

*Grandchildren Megan Niehaus
and Natalie Niehaus, counting
their eggs while Johnny sticks
out his tongue.*

"I can still hear the beautiful Gregorian chant of the monks, O Come, O Come, Emmanuel."

Christmas Memories

From *Niehaus News*, December, 1999/January, 2000

One of my fondest memories of the Christmas Season was when I was in the Seminary at Saint Meinrad. Advent there was a very liturgical season. The first Sunday of Advent came in the last week of November and it was on this Sunday the Advent Wreath with its four candles was blessed. I can still hear the beautiful Gregorian chant of the monks "O Come, O Come, Emmanuel." Each Sunday thereafter, another candle was lit and the growing anticipation of Christmas vacation and going home was on everyone's mind. While at home for Christmas vacation, the seminarians were always asked to serve Midnight Mass. The ceremony really captured the real meaning of Christmas. The lights in the church were turned off and only the candles beautifully illuminated the altar. In the entrance procession, one of the servers would carry the Christ Child to be placed in the crib scene and the organ would play that familiar tune, "O Come, O Come, Emmanuel" as we marched down the aisle.

Over the years we have attended many Midnight Masses with our children to repeat this beautiful memory. Also, our home has always had the Advent Wreath to remind us four weeks before Christmas, of the coming of the Christ Child. One of the traditions was that the oldest child would light the wreath and the youngest would blow it out. As you might imagine there was always an argument, so we finally went in alphabetical order—that was easy, Anne, Butch, Catherine, David and Eric.

This year my wife, Patty, is giving each of our children and their families an Advent Wreath—so that they might carry on this tradition in their family. Our families and our lives have been filled with many blessings. We will have 29 at our Christmas table this year and are looking forward to being with our fourteen grandchildren. We hope you and your family will help bring Christ back into Christmas and maybe listen really close for that familiar chant, "O Come, O Come, Emmanuel."

At our Christmas dinner table is Patty's sister and her husband,
Barbara, and Jerry McGaughey and their son, Scott.

Our grandchildren lighting our traditional Advent Wreath.

Our grandchildren sharing Christmas dinner together.

October 31, 1983

Mr. Bernard Niehaus

100 Lakewood

Vincennes, IN   47591

Dear Bernie:

These are some of my thoughts; some of the details given by Clayton about the lumber
business are not of my recollection.

I do remember that I was a priest at that time, stationed at St. John's in Vincennes
when the business was expanding and I would go down to see Dad and see what progress
was being made. When Francis took over and Dad retired, I could see an upsurge in
business. Francis began immediately to expand the different kinds of sales proper
to a venture of that sort; for example, the sale of paint, some hardware, etc. Dad,
seeing the increase in sales, would remark it would result in an increase in taxes
(Dad was very conscious of taxes in the business), but I think he was very proud of
Francis in the success he was making of the business.

If I remember correctly, Alf was in the business -- but only for a limited time,
inheriting the electrical business from Mr. Freund as his future occupation.

After Francis passed on, Naomi should be admired and praised for carrying on the
operation so successfully until you could finish your schooling at Michigan State.
Like your Dad, you could only see further progress in the business, which sometimes
seemed to give your mother some wonderment.

From then on, the progress made was due to your ingenuity and God's blessing.

Sincerely,

Rev. Fred Niehaus

Fr. Fred

FN:pg

"Father was a man of prayer . . . a reflection of a joyful, peace-filled God-man."

Father Niehaus

From *Niehaus News*, November, 2003

Father Fred Niehaus was born May 5, 1903. This year he would have been 100 years old. He died on March 25, 1992, shortly before his 89th birthday.

Father Niehaus was the sixth of nine children born to Mary and Ben Niehaus. He was born in Vincennes and attended Sacred Heart Grade School. He went to Saint Meinrad for high school, college and theology. He was ordained a priest on June 7, 1927. His first 10 years he served at St. John's in Vincennes, just 2 blocks from where my dad and grandfather (his dad) started Niehaus Planing Mill in 1933. It is from this context that he wrote the letter to me in 1980 about his recollections of the beginning of Niehaus Lumber. My mother tells the story that Father Niehaus often kidded my mom about them opening a peanut factory instead of a planing mill at 10th and Vigo.

After my father died in 1944 (Father Niehaus' brother), my sister (Sonie) and I adopted him as our father. Consequently he spent many holidays and many other special days with our family. On one particular Christmas when I was about nine, I got a new baseball bat as a gift. Father was sitting in his favorite lounge chair with his legs crossed and he told me to hit the bottom of his shoe with my new bat. I scored a home run and he was on crutches for two weeks.

In his many years as a priest, he acquired many titles. He was honored with the rank of Monsignor in 1967. When he became the Dean of the area, his fellow priests dubbed him as the "Jolly Dean." His fellow parish team at St. Anthony's called him "The Boss."

Father was a man of prayer. The mass, the rosary, the breviary, the Bible and spiritual reading were all a part of his daily routine. Card playing, food, and friends helped to keep him wholly human—a reflection of a joyful, peace-filled God-man.

Our family has opened an endowment with the Catholic Foundation that will benefit the parishes he served: St. John's, Vincennes, St. Joseph County, and St. Anthony's in Evansville.

Our Artist Goes to Church

THE REV. FRED NIEHAUS, PASTOR OF THE ST. ANTHONY CATHOLIC CHURCH, 710 FIRST-AV, EVANSVILLE

BEFORE COMING TO EVANSVILLE 8 YEARS AGO, FATHER NIEHAUS SERVED IN VINCENNES (HIS HOME TOWN) FROM 1927 TO 1937 AND LATER THE ST. JOSEPH PARISH, R.R. 4, EVANSVILLE.

ST. ANTHONY IS ATTENDED BY 300 PERSONS.

FATHER NIEHAUS' PRESENT DUTIES HAVE CURTAILED HIS RECREATIONAL ACTIVITIES. THERE WAS A TIME, HOWEVER, DURING HIS STAY AT ST. JOE, WHEN HE WAS KNOWN TO FREQUENTLY TAKE UP THE GUN AND TROD AFIELD FOR RABBITS AND OTHER SMALL GAME.

° LARRY H...

An article published in the Evansville Courier during the time Father Niehaus served as Pastor of St. Anthony's.

Father Niehaus

*Father Niehaus celebrated his
25th year as a priest in 1952.
Bernie Niehaus is carrying the
wheat and grapes.*

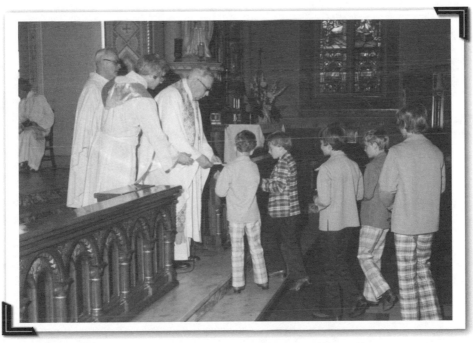

*Father Niehaus celebrating his 50 years as a priest in 1977. Giving communion
to his 5 great-nephews: Eric Niehaus, Michael Glennon, David Niehaus, Danny
Glennon, and Butch Niehaus. Assisting Father Niehaus is Father Ted Temple
and Father Al Niehaus (his nephew).*

"The "Holy Hill"...had a tremendous impact on all who went there."

Saint Meinrad

From *Niehaus News*, October, 2003

I spent three years at Saint Meinrad, from 1951–1954. These were the most formative years of my life. The "Holy Hill," as most alumni call Saint Meinrad, had a tremendous impact on all who went there.

We got up with the bell in the morning at 5:25 with morning prayers and mass at 6:00. We closed the day with Night Silence, Study Hall, and Evening Prayer. This instilled in me a discipline that helped me through college, the Army, and rest of my life.

The many rules of Saint Meinrad were enforced by Disciplinarians. The two I remember the most were Father Amelian and Father Gerard. They each carried little black books in which they kept track of our misbehavings. Father Gerard and I got along great—maybe because my middle name was Gerard.

They certainly kept us busy on the "Holy Hill." We went to classes Monday through Saturday, and had Tuesday and Thursday afternoons off. Father Dunstan, a beloved, jovial monk, was our athletic director and he led us in all the intramural sports. Also, on Tuesday and Thursday afternoons we could sign up to work in the garden, make rosaries with Father Patrick, or work at the Abbey Press. Since I hated gardening work, I chose the Abbey Press and making rosaries. These were fun times keeping busy working for the Lord.

All of our classes were taught by priests. My favorites were Father Pamarus for history, Father Richard for biology, Father Kevin for physics, and Father Marion for Latin. These were college level courses being taught in high school, as I found out, when I got to college and was way ahead of the other students.

One of my most proud achievements at Saint Meinrad was making the Chancel Choir—over one hundred male voices. We sang for all the big celebrations in the Abbey Church, and on one occasion, we gave a concert in Louisville for the highlight of the year.

I owe Saint Meinrad a lot, for it was the best thing that happened to me.

Family brings Sunday picnic. Seminarians are left to right: Bernie Niehaus, Larry Jaussad, Charlie Bowman, David Mulheron, Clarence Thomas.

Bernie Niehaus - 1954. Third class at Saint Meinrad Seminary.

A visit to Saint Meinrad - My Aunt Ella Mae Hunter and her twin sons, Larry and Terry Hunter.

Sunday afternoon visit to Monte Cassino - 1952. Naomi Niehaus (my mother) and Viola Fuller (my aunt).

The "Holy Hill"—a view of Saint Meinrad Archabbey Church.

Chapter 6
The Niehaus Lumber "Gallery"
—A photo history

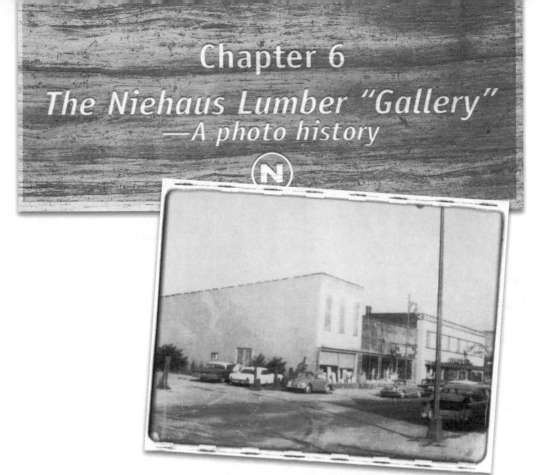

- *The Early Years*

- *Niehaus Lumber — 1950–1980*

- *Wholesale Building Materials — 1970–2000*

- *The New Home Center — 1995*

- *Center Hardware and WBM; Big Bucks*

The early years

1943—Bernie Niehaus at age 6. During the war lumber was hard to find and Bernie went on several mill trips to the south with his father and grandfather to buy poplar.

Francis Niehaus, Bernie's father, co-founder of Niehaus Lumber.

Ben Niehaus, Bernie's grandfather, and co-founder of Niehaus Lumber Company in 1933.

Niehaus Lumber Company building undergoing facelift in 1953.

The old railroad spur that ran along the parking lot at Niehaus Lumber on Main Street.

Niehaus Lumber Company—taken in the 1950's.

Old time lumber shed with lumber bins and a catwalk for upper bins. Lumber had to be put away by hand—a very time-consuming chore.

The early years

In the late 50's, trusses were handmade in the mill at Niehaus Lumber.

The very first pre-made, prefinished cabinet display to go in Niehaus Lumber. Prior to 1960, all cabinets were handmade in our mill.

Bernie Niehaus presenting service awards to three long-time employees. Left: Louie Keller - 20 years, Clayton Miller - 35 years, and Tom Chesser - 43 years.

In the early days, nails were sold by the pound and stored in a large revolving bin and measured out on a scale and bagged up for the customer.

Niehaus Cash-Away Lumber takes on a new look after renovation in 1964.

Niehaus Lumber 1950-1980's

Vi Fuller and Agnes Bastin, sales ladies in the Paint and Appliance Departments during the 1960's.

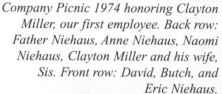

Company Picnic 1974 honoring Clayton Miller, our first employee. Back row: Father Niehaus, Anne Niehaus, Naomi Niehaus, Clayton Miller and his wife, Sis. Front row: David, Butch, and Eric Niehaus.

Niehaus Cash-Away, 1023 Main St., recently completed purchase of additional property for expansion from the Pennsylvania Railroad. Bernie Niehaus (left), Bill Wiechman of the Pennsylvania Railroad and Jerry McGaughey, railroad attorney, negotiated sale of land and buildings by the railroad. Niehaus will have an additional 27,000 square feet adjacent to their buildings between Main and Vigo streets. The property bought from the railroad includes the freight warehouse, the parking area now being used by Niehaus and approximately 20,000 square feet of lumber storage area. Niehaus will be able to unload six carloads of building materials at a time, two at dock level and four at ground level, with the new property.

Octave Quinett and Clayton Miller's sons barbecuing chicken for the picnic.

Employees socializing at the picnic. Larry Pipher, Marilyn Costello, Ella Harsha, Vanita Cofer, and in the back are Jim Hand and Kelly Updike.

Niehaus Home Center in the 80's.

Niehaus Lumber 1950-1980's

The old lumber shed was torn down to make way for a new 15,000 square foot drive-thru lumber and building materials warehouse.

1975 - The new warehouse going up. The drive-thru facility was designed by C.S. Lorimer from the U.S.G. Company.

1975 - after the new warehouse was complete, the contractor customers were invited to a grand opening. Bernie Niehaus and Naomi Niehaus greet guests.

Tom Chesser and Bernie Niehaus posing in front of a photo board commemerating the company's 50th anniversary celebration.

Photo of Niehaus Cash-Away sales force as appeared in Vincennes Sun-Commercial August 20, 1968. Shown are: Bernie Niehaus, Vi Fuller, Alan Sievers, Lowell Cockrum, Agnes Bastin, Tom Chesser, Paul Cox, Chuck Tewalt and Eldon Campbell.

Wholesale Building Materials 1970 – 2000

Brian Smith, Manager of the Top Shop.

Todd Donovan, Aristokraft Sales Manager, Wholesale Building Materials.

The Door Component Plant was the first building constructed on a 40 acre plot located on Elkhorn Road in Vincennes. It was later named Wholesale Building Materials and became the home of the Aristokraft Cabinet Distribution center, door mill, Karran USA, the Top Shop and corporate headquarters.

The early days of the door mill where pre-hung doors were built to order.

WBM employees in the Engineeered Lumber Department receive an award for sales and excellence. Left to right: Connie Lockhart, Clete Yochum, Eric Feagley, and John Harrison.

Don Pea - Corporate Projects Manager, for Niehaus Companies Incorporated.

Jerry Burch, Sales Manager for Wholesale Building Materials.

Niehaus Companies Accounting Staff: Left to right: Dana Smith, Helen Smith, Stephanie Zachary, Jean Fox, Carla Winegart and Mike Adams (CFO).

WBM 1970 – 2000

Wholesale Building Materials as it looks today.

Mike Worland, manager of the door mill located at WBM in Vincennes.

Roy Roach, 29-year employee who has worked in the door mill since the beginning.

Debi Moyes, 25-year employee with WBM in Vincennes.

Brian Lett – Operations Manager at Wholesale Building Materials.

Tony Jamero is the Network Administrator for Niehaus Companies.

Kim Smith – Manager of lumber and commodities division has been with our company for 28 years and served in many capacities from loader to yard manager.

Eric, David and Butch Niehaus in front of the new walls being constructed for new accounting offices at WBM.

The New Home Center - 1995

The first stages of the 1995 remodeling of Niehaus Home Center.

Bernie Niehaus posing with Jeff Gordon's car on display at Niehaus Home Center during a special promotion.

The new facade is progressing in the remodeling project.

Boyd Small is honored at his retirement. Left to right: Boyd, Phil Wehrman, Mike Cavender, David Niehaus and Mary Edgin.

Niehaus women employees attend Christmas party and gift exchange. Left to right: Ginger Welton, Sharon English, Cathy Yochum, Mary Edgin, and Chris Morine.

Mark Ashcraft, Bill and Janet Stevens at the annual company family picnic.

The third and final stage in completing the remodeling of Niehaus Home Center.

The New Home Center - 1995

David Niehaus showing off a midget racer on display for a special promotion.

Dan Martens, manager of the Contractor Division at Niehaus Home Center.

Phil Wehrman, Manager at Niehaus Home Center.

Wayne Sullivan, Manager of the Installation Department at Niehaus Home Center.

Phil Cutshall, Home Decor Manager, and Lisa Litherland, Paint Dept. Manager

Kitchen and bath designers,
Sue Fox and Ginger Welton.

Phil Wehrman, manager, holds training meeting
for employees.

Taken at an ILBSA
awards ceremony
where Niehaus Home
Center took first place
in six categories of
competition. Left to
right: Danny
Harrington, Phil
Wehrman, Kathy
McCreary, Bernie
Niehaus, Sherry
Cummins and David
Niehaus.

Keith Fox, Contractor
Salesman.

Bernie Niehaus in front of giant flag display made of units of
2 x 4's and painted to celebrate Flag Day and the 4th of July.

Center Hardware & WBM - *St. Louis, Nashville* *and Big Bucks* - *Robinson and Terre Haute*

Center Hardware - purchased and renovated in 1992, was a complete hardware store and garden center, located at Niblack and Washington Avenue.

Center Hardware was purchased and renovated in 1992 by the Niehaus family. However, just a few short months after the grand opening, a fire of unknown origin broke out and completely destroyed the building and its contents. It was decided not to rebuild at this location, but to remodel and expand at the Main Street business, which is now Niehaus Home Center.

*Brian Childs, Manager of the
St. Louis division of Wholesale
Building Materials.*

*Tim Boone, Manager of the
Big Buck Pro Building
Center in Terre Haute, IN.*

*Larry McCoy, Manager of
the Big Buck Building
Center in Robinson, Illinois*

*Don Kirby, Manager
of the Nashville,
Tennessee division of
Wholesale Building
Materials.*

*Sherry Cummins,
Advertising-Marketing
Manager for Niehaus
Companies, posing
with the Pink Panther,
during the Center
Hardware Grand
Opening celebration.*

Ed's Discount Warehouse - located in Robinson, Illinois. Ed's is an outlet for all less-than-perfect merchandise accumulated from the six business locations in Niehaus Companies.

Mark Webster, Todd Donovan, Spokesperson Linda Kruse, Paul Martin, Gary Owen, Chaz Clary and Eric Niehaus pose at their Karran Sink display booth at the National Kitchen and Bath Show in Orlando, Florida. Karran USA, a division of Niehaus Companies, is the national distributor of the Karran solid surface sinks and whirlpools.

Index of Subjects and Photos

E

Easter, 159
Eck, Stan, 58
Edgin, Mary K., 58, 66, 189
Ed's Discount Warehouse, 194
Egbert, Bill, 58, 66
Eli Stout Print Shop, 110
Elk's Country Club, 87, 129
English, Sharon, 58, 189
Eubank, Troy, 58
Extra Mile Awards, 57-8, 61

F

Feagley, Eric, 58, 66, 185
Flaget Elementary School, 62
Flickner, Doug, 58
Florida, 99
Forbes, Richard, 12
Fort Knox Site II, 110
Fort Myers, FL, 101
Fort Sackville, 109, 111
Foster, Rev. Pat, 95, 97
Fox, Jean, 58, 66, 185
Fox, Keith, 66, 114, 191
Fox, Sue, 66, 191
Franz, Dean, 58, 66
Frenz, John, 134
Frisz, Bob, 66
Fuller, Bert and Viola, 137, 173, 180, 183
Fuller, Millard, 125
Futaba of America, 135

G

Gaines, Ron, 66
Gardner, George, 19
Gerdemann, Steve, 66
Glennon, Danny, 169

Glennon, Michael, 169
Goldman, Jack, 58
Good Samaritan Hospital, 135
Grantham, Shannon, 58, 66
Gregg Park, 117-19
Gregg, John, 134
Gross, T. Scott, 49
Grostefon, Kevin, 66
Grouseland, 110

H

Haase, Art, 123
Habitat for Humanity, 125-27
Hageman, Bill, 58
Hall, Tracy, 58
Hand, Jim, 181
Harrington, Danny, 58, 66, 191
Harrison, Deb, 58
Harrison, John, 66, 185
Harrison, William Henry, 109-10
Harsha, Ella, 181
Hartigan, Mike, 142-43
Henry, Rick, 66
Hensley, Carl, 65, 127
Hillcrest Hospital, 23
Hunter, Ella Mae, 173
Hunter, Larry, 173
Hunter, Terry, 173

I

Indiana Territory, 109

J

Jamero, Tony, 187
Jaussad, Larry, 172
Jones, Michael, 66
Jordon, Bernice, 66